MEXICO
THE VEGETARIAN TABLE

MEXICO

THE VEGETARIAN TABLE

BY VICTORIA WISE

PHOTOGRAPHY BY DEBORAH JONES

FOOD STYLING BY SANDRA COOK

CHRONICLE BOOKS · SAN FRANCISCO

DEDICATION

❁

For Rick and Jenan who

with constancy, grace, and great good humor

so often dine on a meal of my recipes

Library of Congress Cataloging-in-Publication Data:
Wise, Victoria.
    The vegetarian table: Mexico/by Victoria Wise:
photography by Deborah Jones.
        p. cm.
    Includes index.
    ISBN 0-8118-0475-5
    1. Vegetarian cookery. 2. Cookery, Mexican. I. Title.
TX837.W56   1995
641.5′636—dc20   94-13125
                                                    CIP

Book Design: Louise Fili Ltd.
Design Assistants: Leah Lococo and Tonya Hudson
Prop Stylist: Sara Slavin
Photo Assistant: Jeri Jones
Food Stylist Assistant: Allyson Levy
Props provided by San Francisco stores Zonal and Hecho A Mano

Printed in Hong Kong.

Distributed in Canada by Raincoast Books,
8680 Cambie Street, Vancouver, B.C. V6P 6M9

10 9 8 7 6 5 4 3 2 1

Chronicle Books
275 Fifth Street
San Francisco, CA 94103

CONTENTS

✹

INTRODUCTION 6

Earth Tones and Radiant Flavors

GLOSSARY OF INGREDIENTS 8

The Culinary Conquest of the Old World by the New

Notes to the Cook on Some Special Preparations

CHAPTER ONE

Salsas & Condiments 17

CHAPTER TWO

Tortilla Cuisine 43

CHAPTER THREE

Soups 67

CHAPTER FOUR

Pasta, Rice & Beans 83

CHAPTER FIVE

Salads & Vegetables 103

CHAPTER SIX

Sweets 129

INDEX 150

TABLE OF EQUIVALENTS 155

INTRODUCTION

❋

EARTH TONES AND RADIANT FLAVORS

T HE MEXICAN EARTH, WARMED BY THE SUN, WATERED FROM THE HEAVENS, AND PROTECTED BY CHICOMECOATL, A MOST GENEROUS GODDESS OF VEGETATION, GAVE TO PEOPLE A BOUNTIFUL HARVEST. The potato, tomato, corn, summer squash, winter squash—and their blossoms and seeds—avocado, pineapple, chocolate, and vanilla, the peanut, pecan, cashew, all the beans save one, and every capsicum, from bell peppers to chilies, all came from the New World. These crops, cultivated since ancient times, provided the ingredients for the daily fare of the Mexican table long before Columbus planted a Spanish flag in the West Indies and later European followers arrived under sundry other banners on the Atlantic and Pacific shores of the Americas.

The invaders, unwelcome and reviled by the native population, nonetheless brought desirable goods for the table. In particular, the Spanish imported wheat flour and rice (hence the numerous *arroz* and pasta dishes, or "dry soups," called *sopas secas*), the Old World fava, or broad bean, all the peas we eat, including lentils and chickpeas, melons, oranges, limes, almonds, sesame seeds, olives and olive oil, garden onions, and capers, cinnamon, and mustard for seasoning.

Throughout a long history of tribulation and changing power in Mexico, the new foods from Europe became solidly incorporated into the native cuisine. Cooking and eating assumed the role of a tempering link between the many factions. Outside the range of battle, in the safety of the house, the foodstuffs of both agricultures came together in the pots and pans of the New World kitchens. Ingredients, styles, and techniques were interchanged, culinary secrets were traded and shared, and in time, a new cuisine emerged.

Today, the stock of ingredients in Mexican cooking draws from the huge store of these two culinarily rich cultures. With such a full measure of ingredients and wealth of flavors, it's easy to see how Mexican cooking easily adapts to the vegetarian table. Both the pre-Columbian and Spanish traditions rely heavily on vegetables, grains, and fruits. In addition, the parallel culinary paths share another, less obvious, advantage for the vegetarian eater. Health and well-being for anyone relies on having a balanced diet that provides enough carbohydrates, protein, minerals, and vitamins to sustain life.

For the vegetarian diet, which eliminates meat, poultry, usually fish, and in the most severe interpretation, eggs as well, the problem is to garner enough whole protein. Mexican cooking provides a solution in two ways: While the Spanish brought a protein boon of cheese and other dairy products from their animal husbandry, the native Mexican tradition contributed a special source of its own.

Long ago, the natives of Mexico fortuitously discovered how to derive whole protein from corn. By boiling dried corn kernels with lime, originally from wood ash, not only did they loosen the hulls and ready the kernels easily to grind for corn flour, they also chanced upon a magic chemistry that turns corn into a more nutritious food of complete protein and extra mineral content. The lime-treated corn, called *nixtamal,* became the staple of a burgeoning population, and corn itself became idolized as the source of life. Many deities, both male and female, arose in ancient Mexican mythology and religion to watch over and bless its various stages of development, from the initial budding to the early gathering of tender ears for fresh eating to the full crop harvest and on through the drying stage. Corn remains the major food source in Mexico.

Later, rice was introduced to Mexican cooking, either by the Spanish or by Chinese immigrants, it's not certain which. Coupled with the native beans in another happy food pairing, rice and beans provided an alternative complete protein. Since both rice and beans are products that can be stored through their nongrowing season, the pair added a second, keepable, complete food to the Mexican diet, and being as economically viable as the corn staples, they came to be greatly exploited.

All in all, Mexican cuisine today is robust, varied, and creative and lends itself easily to vegetarian eating. Good cooking, in any case, is a living art, flexible and accommodating to the new as well as the old. Following that pathway, I take lively liberties with classic preparations and compositions. On the one hand, I rely on the glorious variety of healthful ancient staples of both the Old and New Worlds for the stuff of the meal—corn, beans, rice—and complement and expand the vegetable components with tomatoes, chilies, fresh greens, squashes, and the onions and garlic that pervade the world's cooking. On the other hand, I find many dishes in the established cuisine too labor intensive. These were, after all, devised when women spent the day from dawn to dusk and into the night tending the garden, harvesting, preparing, and serving food, and beginning preparations for the next day again before retiring. While I frequently spend the time to stew up a pot of beans, prepare a *mole*, or turn out festive tamales, I do so to have stock on hand for a few days or to treat my friends and family.

Also, I find many classic dishes too fat laden. For this collection of recipes, I eliminated lard altogether, and do as I do in my own kitchen, substitute olive oil, with an occasional indulgence in a pat or two of butter. Instead of meat or chicken stock, I use vegetable stock, wine, or olive oil to moisten and round out flavors. I add cheese, nuts, olives, and fresh herb garnishes to complete and finish a dish.

With these provisos—quicker preparations, lighter fare, no animal ingredients except for eggs and dairy products—I think the following collection of recipes reflects a harmonious compendium of the old, the new, and the modern, and I've made it easy, I hope, for you to adapt traditional Mexican cooking to your vegetarian table. *Buen provecho!*

GLOSSARY OF INGREDIENTS

✸

THE CULINARY CONQUEST OF THE OLD WORLD BY THE NEW

SEAFARING EXPLORERS OF THE FIFTEENTH AND SIXTEENTH CENTURIES SET SAIL SEEKING WEALTH BEYOND THEIR KNOWN HORIZONS. As legend promised, they expected to find gold and an abundance of precious spices. Instead, over the horizon, across the ocean, and halfway around the world, they found a storehouse they hadn't dreamed of: a thriving agriculture of golden goods for the table.

That was late in the fifteenth century. Throughout the sixteenth century, the seeds of the New World foods traversed the oceans. Transported and disseminated by seafarers and explorers as they carried on their voyages of discovery, New World seeds were planted and took hold globally. They sprouted up everywhere, and their products set the culinary world ablaze. By the seventeenth century, New World foods had transformed the pantries and kitchens of the Old World forever.

From place to place around the world, selections occurred, it's true, probably determined by agricultural possibilities as well as by local taste. For instance, tomatoes never caught on in Oriental cuisine, though in southern Europe you can't imagine the cooking without them. In northern Europe, the Irish adopted the potato as their own, so much so that many people don't know there were no potatoes across the Atlantic until after Columbus set sail. Then again, many Asian cooks have a strong affection for hot peppers, though in Europe almost no one does, with the notable exceptions of the Hungarians with their hot paprika and the southern Italians and Sicilians with their *peperoncini.* With few exceptions, outside the Americas corn is mostly relegated to fodder and not thought of as a table food, though northern Italians and Rumanians grind it coarse and cook the tasty mush they call polenta and *mamaliga.* Beans, both the fresh ones we call green beans and the many varieties of dried ones, show up everywhere except in the Orient where New World beans never displaced the already established and nourishing mung and soy. Exceptionally, vanilla and chocolate were embraced almost everywhere, and they perfume the world.

Overall, today New World foods are by and large familiar and available. Whether of European, Asian, or African descent, cooks have incorporated many, if not all, the larder staples of the Mexican vegetarian table into their dishes. Some of the less common ingredients, such as tomatillos, certain chilies, the occasional herb or spice, you can find canned or dried if not fresh. Following is a brief glossary to guide you. Some of the more esoteric ingredients, such as jícama, squash blossoms, and tamarind, are described in the individual recipes calling for them.

✸

CHILIES

Close cousins of the sweet bell peppers—often called by their generic name, *Capsicum,* to distinguish them from the pepperberry spice, *Piper nigrum*—chilies are the spicy branch of the family. The range and variety of chili peppers is astounding, if not befuddling, especially if you are not familiar with them. Don't be intimidated. There *are* taste differences, but

with a few pointers, you can substitute one chili for another and adjust the amount to suit your own tolerance. Generally speaking, the main difference in taste and use is between the fresh and the dried. Fresh chilies are usually hotter and lend a vegetable flavor to the dish. Dried chilies are milder as a rule and can be considered more of a spice ingredient.

❁

FRESH CHILIES

ANAHEIMS. Sometimes called California chilies in Mexico, these are five to six inches long, narrow, and tapering to a point. They are mild, sometimes with a little heat. They are mostly green, ripening to orange and sometimes red. Anaheims are the type normally found canned as whole green chilies.

HABANEROS. Used throughout the Yucatan and Caribbean, sometimes called Scotch Bonnet after their shape, which resembles a nineteenth-century lady's hat. These are one to two inches long, roundish with a pointy tip, green to yellow to bright orange-red. Habaneros are a favorite of mine for the fruity, fresh taste that underpins the heat, but because they are exceedingly hot, even relentlessly so to the uninitiated, I don't call for them in these recipes. Feel free to substitute them for jalapeños or serranos any time.

JALAPEÑOS. Jalapeños are the everyman's chili pepper of Mexican cooking and can be used wherever chopped fresh chilies are called for. They are one to one and a half inches long, narrow and pointed, green ripening to red, and they range from mild to rather hot. You can interchange them with the smaller serrano or the same size, yellow güero chilies or substitute canned jalapeños, usually put up in a mild brine with some herbs and carrot and onion slices.

POBLANOS. These are about five inches long, the size of medium bell peppers but with a pointed tip; they are dark green, mild to hot. Dried poblanos are called pasillas.

SERRANOS. Tiny, three-quarter to one inch long, quite thin and pointed, sometimes ripening to bright red, these are mild to hot. Use them as you would jalapeños.

❁

DRIED CHILIES

ANCHOS. Oblong in shape, these are three and a half to five inches long, two to three inches wide, deep red-brown, mild and musky to warm in taste. Anchos are my dried chili of choice. They are not offensively hot, even to children, and they have the added advantage of pureeing smoothly into a sauce without your having to scrape the pulp away from the peel.

ARBOLS AND JAPONES. These small dried red chili peppers are thin and long, from three-quarter to one and a half inches and quite hot. They are often used for chili flakes. Use them wherever you'd like the dried spice taste of hot chilies.

CHIPOTLES. Special unto themselves, chipotles are smoke-dried jalapeños. They are one to two inches long, one-half inch wide, amber brown with hints of red, and quite hot. You can purchase them canned in brine or dry in packages.

PASILLAS. Dried green poblanos, these are mild yet deep-flavored, five to seven inches long, thinner and more tapered than anchos, and a darker brownish red. They're a substitute for anchos, though pasillas make a less smooth, stringy puree for sauces if they're not strained.

POWDERED CHILI. The flavor of a particular chili powder is determined by the kind of dried chili from which it is ground. Chili powder, especially the small bottles we commonly find on spice racks in grocery stores, is often mixed with cumin, salt, and other spices to make an all-purpose seasoning powder more akin to a *mole*. If you can, purchase pure chili powders—ancho, New Mexico, Colorado, or some other chili—not mixed with other seasonings.

✺
CORN

MASA, MASA HARINA, AND CORNMEAL: A BRIEF HISTORY. For corn tortillas, and tamales as well, the stuff of the dough is corn, first dried, then boiled with slaked lime, then hulled and ground. Called *nixtamal*, from the Aztec word for the wood ash that provided the lime component in pre-Hispanic times, this special corn supplied protein, vitamins, and minerals beyond what corn can deliver in its natural, untreated state. *Nixtamal* became the basic food of the Americas. It was mixed with water to make a wet dough called *masa* which was patted into tortillas, shaped into tamales, or cooked into gruel for breakfast, lunch, and dinner. But this simple *masa* was very perishable.

At some point, people figured out how to preserve the *nixtamal* for longer keeping. They further dried the lime-treated corn and ground it a little finer so that it would rehydrate more easily for the *masa* that was their staff of life. Now, it was not so perishable and would keep through a cold winter and dry spring. An extra advantage was that it was more compact and lighter, better for storing and transporting. It was not, perhaps, as tasty as the fresh stuff, but it was still food, nutritious food, still *nixtamal*. Thus evolved *masa harina*, or corn flour.

Decades later, when there were wider choices for protein in the New World and nutrition needs could be met in other ways from cattle husbandry and alternative grains (wheat and rice), food became perhaps a little less momentary and people didn't have to work so hard at refining corn into a sustenance food. With plenty, the dried corn could be ground straightaway, without previous lime soaking and hulling, to make flour or meal for porridge or biscuits or mush. That's how we got our cornmeal, eventually the Italians their polenta, and most recently, the Zimbabweans their *sadza*.

You can purchase *masa harina* (corn flour) for making tortillas in most supermarkets. Quaker and Maseca brands are both excellent. If you have a specialty Mexican market nearby, you can purchase the *masa* dough freshly made and ready to press or roll out.

✺
HERBS

The perennial herbs of slatey landscapes are the seasoning of Mexican dishes. Most are familiar—sage, marjoram, oregano, bay. Epazote and *hoja santa* stand out as peculiar to Mexican cooking. Sometimes called wormseed, epazote is also native in Europe and North America but little used as a culinary herb elsewhere than in Mexico. It has a musty, pungent flavor and is best used fresh rather than dried. Marjoram makes an acceptable substitute. *Hoja santa*, native to Mexico, is a bush herb with large leaves of mild aniselike flavor that are used to flavor fish and wrap tamales. It, too, loses its punch when dried, but you can simulate its taste with a tiny pinch of anise seed.

Garden herbs that must be replanted annually or coaxed through winter and watered during the dry summer months, like dill, tarragon, and basil, are not customary in Mexican cooking. Cilantro, a member of the parsley family, is the exception. The fresh leaf is widely used in Mexican and Asian cooking, though European cooks prefer the seed of the plant, called coriander. Some cannot abide the taste of cilantro, which they find overpowering. If you are one, substitute parsley.

The spices for Mexican cooking are probably already stocked on your shelves: cinnamon, cloves, nutmeg, maybe allspice. Aside from dried chilies and chili powder, which you may or may not have on hand, the only oddity is achiote, an important ingredient, especially of Yucatan cooking. As powder, ground from the seeds of the annatto bush, it is usually mixed with other herbs and spices to make a seasoning paste called a *mole*. Achiote is not forceful as a flavor; rather, it fills the same culinary niche as turmeric and saffron—a mildly fragrant coloring agent. It lends an appealing orange-red hue to sauces and marinades. Added to rice, it turns the dish an eye-pleasing ochre color. You can find achiote paste packaged in brick form, or, purchase annatto seeds, grind and mix them with a pinch each of ground cinnamon, cumin, and clove, dried oregano, and salt; moisten the mixture with a splash of vinegar. Or substitute a half-and-half mixture of sweet paprika and mild chili powder.

※

OTHER BASIC SEASONINGS

NUTS AND SEEDS. Since pre-Columbian times, nuts and seeds have been a notable element of Mexican cooking. They include such true nuts as the almond, pecan, cashew, and walnut; seeds like pumpkin and sesame; and the New World peanut, a legume. All are liberally used to thicken, flavor, and embellish stews, sauces, and sweets.

OIL. Other than lard, which is pervasively used for frying, baking, and tortilla-making, cooking fats are not forceful tastes in Mexican cooking. In this book, as at home, I ignore the norm, never use lard, and always opt for the more strongly flavored oil of either peanut or olive. Safflower and corn oils, while more typical, are too mild and watery for my taste.

ACID. The acid ingredient, whether as citrus or vinegar, can be loosely described as the sour taste in cooking. The sour is a primary component on the palette of flavors in any particular cuisine, and tastes vary widely: Some like it sharp, some like it soft, some like it not at all. In Mexican cooking, sour is a gentle element. It appears as lime rather than the more acerbic lemon, as a low-acid fruit-based vinegar rather than the sharper wine vinegars or deep, assertive balsamic vinegars I most often use to suit my own taste. It's easy enough to make fruit vinegar if you care to. Apple cider or rice wine vinegars both make good substitutes for it in the recipes in this book.

※

FRUIT VINEGAR

MAKES 6 CUPS

1 cup (packed) dark brown sugar

1½ cups Mexican beer, such as Carta Blanca or Corona

8 cups water

1 overripe but not blackened banana, unpeeled and cut in half crosswise

2 sweet apples, such as Golden Delicious, unpeeled and halved

Peel with ½-inch of pulp attached of half a ripe medium pineapple

Place the sugar, beer, and water in a gallon glass or heavy, clear plastic jar and stir to dissolve the sugar. Rinse the fruit and add to the jar. Loosely cover the jar with plastic wrap, leaving space for gases to escape as the liquid ferments. Set the jar aside at room temperature in a sunny place for 3 to 5 weeks, depending on the weather and ripeness of the fruit, until the liquid is amber in color with a thick, milky-white layer on top.

Spoon off the white layer and save it to start another batch of vinegar. Strain the liquid through cheesecloth into a clean container and then funnel it into a bottle. Cork the bottle and use the vinegar as you need it. It improves with age.

NOTES TO THE COOK ON SOME SPECIAL PREPARATIONS

When approaching cookery in the Mexican style, it is helpful to know a few special techniques that are typically used to ready certain ingredients for a dish. These include the preparation of bell peppers and chilies, whether fresh or dried, large or small; tomatoes; tomatillos; nuts and seeds; and spices.

PEPPERS

LARGE FRESH PEPPERS. In Mexican cooking, the large capsicums, both chilies and bells, are always peeled, seeded, and deveined before proceeding with a recipe. To do this, first roast or char their skins loose with high heat. You can either place the peppers in a preheated 450 degree F. oven, or on a grill rack directly above a hot charcoal fire, or under a broiler, or over a gas burner. Turn them after ten minutes and continue roasting until the skins blister and blacken in spots all around, five to fifteen minutes more, depending on the heat level and method you are using. Remove the peppers from the heat and cover them with a cloth or paper towel to create a steaming effect. When they are cool enough to handle, peel off the skins with your fingers. Finally, pull off the stems and scrape away the seeds and white veins from inside. Cut and use the peppers as directed in the recipe.

SMALL FRESH CHILIES. Small fresh chilies are sometimes roasted and peeled, but just as often, or maybe more usually, they are incorporated freshly chopped into a dish. This is how I always use them. As a rule, I don't bother to seed them because I don't mind the look of the seeds in the dish, and I don't find removing the seeds particularly softens the heat, as some people believe. The exception is when the small chilies are somewhat large, and hence extra seedy, and I am using them for a finishing touch that should be refined in appearance. The seeds of dried chilies are not discarded. They are saved for spicing another dish, if not the one at hand. These considerations are reflected in the recipe instructions.

LARGE DRIED CHILIES. Anchos, pasillas, and the like are either soaked to soften them for grinding or pureeing or thinly sliced straightaway and quickly fried to toast them. In either case, they are traditionally stemmed and seeded, though I sometimes don't fuss.

SMALL DRIED CHILIES. Arbols and japones are stemmed, sometimes seeded and sometimes not, then halved, or chopped, or left whole, depending on the dish.

For all chilies, fresh or dried, there are three additional points to keep in mind:

- When handling chilies, take care not to touch your eyes or mouth. The oils of chili peppers can easily "burn" delicate skin tissue.
- If you have sensitive skin, protect your hands with rubber gloves when preparing chilies.
- In case you've overfired your dish with enthusiasm and/or too hot a chili, the best antidote I've found is to take a large swig or two of milk to soothe the mouth and calm the fire rather than scrambling around the kitchen trying to dilute the heat factor with additional ingredients (you can't, really). If you have guests, caution them and have a pitcher of milk and perhaps an extra-high stack of tortillas ready. Forewarned is forearmed.

TOMATOES. Most typically in Mexican cooking, tomatoes are peeled after charring on a *comal* (Mexican stovetop grill). This method adds a roasted taste as well as splits the skins for easy peeling. You can peel tomatoes several other ways: Char them on a grill over a hot fire or roast them on a baking sheet in a hot oven, just until the skins crack open. Or drop them into a pot of rapidly boiling water, count to twenty, and drain them in a colander; set aside until cool enough to handle. Whatever the method, when cool, remove the skins with your fingers. Usually, the tomatoes are then halved and the seeds are scooped out before proceeding with the recipe.

To save time, modern preparations often omit peeling the tomatoes altogether. If you choose to use the tomatoes unpeeled, simply chop or puree them as indicated in the recipe. Or halve the tomatoes and scoop out the seeds into a bowl to collect the juices. Strain out the seeds and use the juices along with the tomato pulp.

TOMATILLOS. Tomatillos are closely related to tomatoes, and indeed are sometimes called "membrane tomatoes" after the papery, husklike leaves that encase the firm, green fruit. Tomatillos haven't captured the affection of the rest of the world as tomatoes have, but their tart, fresh taste is widely appreciated in Mexican cooking, especially for salsas and sauces. I especially like them simmered with onions to make a sweet-and-sour vegetable stew to accompany rice or bean dishes or fill a tortilla.

To prepare fresh tomatillos, pull off the papery outer leaves and the stems. Rinse the tomatillos to remove the stickiness.

CANNED TOMATILLOS. In a pinch, you can substitute canned tomatillos when fresh ones are not available. Drain them and use right away. It isn't necessary to parboil canned tomatillos as they have already been through the process. If the recipe calls for parboiling fresh tomatillos, reserve the liquid from the can to use in place of the parboiling liquid the recipe calls for.

NUTS AND SEEDS. Whether used whole, chopped, or ground, nuts and seeds are always toasted to release their flavor before being included in a dish. You can toast nuts and seeds in an ungreased skillet over medium-high heat or in a microwave. Since the timing differs depending on the kind of nut or seed and the amount called for, instructions are given individually in each recipe.

SPICES. A special trick of flavor-conscious cooks, and one customarily employed in Mexican cooking, is to toast the spices. Whether whole, coarsely ground, or powdered, the spices called for are mixed together and stirred in an ungreased skillet over medium-high heat until their aroma is redoubled. The mixture is finely ground in a *metate*, or Mexican stone mortar, or spice grinder, then added to the dish. In the interest of streamlining techniques, I did not include this step in the recipes in this book. If you would like to take the time to toast and grind the spices to order, your dish will have that extra depth and breadth of flavor that signifies careful cooking, and your Mexican vegetarian dishes will enjoy special-request status.

chapter one

SALSAS &
CONDIMENTS

SETTING THE TABLE

✹

PERFECTION DISCOVERED IN TEOTITLAN DEL VALLE

IN ANY CUISINE, SETTING THE TABLE INVOLVES PUTTING OUT THE SALT AND PEPPER AS A PRELUDE TO THE MEAL. FROM THERE, THE FORMS VARY WIDELY. The salt may be in the form of NaCl crystals, more or less finely ground, as we and the English and Europeans do or soy sauce, as on an Oriental table. The pepper can be black peppercorns, already ground or served in a table mill for grinding fresh on the spot, or chili pepper, such as the chili flakes of the Italian table or the chili-flavored oils of the Chinese. Often the salt and pepper are combined, as in the hot and salty lemon or lime pickles of Indian and Korean cooking or the salsas, condiments, and chili salt of the Mexican table.

Once, in Teotitlan del Valle, Oaxaca, Mexico, I felicitously stumbled upon the perfect table setting. In that Zapotec village where craft and artistry are woven together into rugs, shawls, wall hangings, amusing objects, and the food of dreams, I enjoyed a most memorable meal at the Restaurant Abagail. Its perfection came from freshness and a deceptive ease—tradition unfettered by stale ritual, combined with a great deal of caprice but no flim-flam. On the table were a plate of fresh lime wedges, a small bowl of toasted pumpkin seeds (*pepitas*), another of very pure guacamole—only ripe avocado mashed with a little minced onion and cilantro, nothing more—accompanied with the thinnest of corn tortillas and a tiny pottery saltcellar of fragrant chili salt to sprinkle on the food as we would. These were the salutations to the meal. As we sat waiting in full sight of the open kitchen, though hunger preyed, there was no doubt of hospitality and the satisfaction soon to come, and there was no disappointment. This chapter begins with the table dishes I found so perfect in Teotitlan del Valle and goes on to include other spicy, savory salsas and sauces of Mexican cooking, perfect greetings all.

CHILI SALT

✹

MAKES ½ CUP

SEASONED SALTS ARE A SPECIAL LOVE OF ANYONE WHO LIKES TO COOK. THE ALCHEMIST/ARTIST IN YOU COMES TO THE FORE WHEN YOU BLEND YOUR OWN SALT AND SPICE MIXTURE TO HAVE IN A CELLAR FOR A TABLE SEASONING OR TO STIR INTO A COOKED DISH. MADE IN VERY SMALL AMOUNTS, THE MIXTURE STAYS AROMATIC AND YOU CAN USE IT UP BEFORE THE FRAGRANCE DIES. FOR TASTE, IT'S IMPORTANT TO HAVE A GOOD-QUALITY SALT, NEITHER TOO COARSE NOR TOO FINE NOR CUT WITH ADDITIVES FOR FREE FLOW, AS MANY COMMERCIAL PACKAGED SALTS ARE.

Mix together all the ingredients. Use right away or store in an airtight jar for up to several weeks.

¼ cup sea salt
¼ cup pure chili powder
1 teaspoon cayenne
⅛ teaspoon ground cloves
⅛ teaspoon dried oregano, crumbled

GUACAMOLE

❋

MAKES 2 CUPS

AN AVOCADO IS AT PERFECTION WHEN (1) IT STARTS LIFE AS A HASS; (2) IT HAS BEEN TREATED WELL AND NOT BRUISED SO THAT IT CAN RIPEN WITHOUT BLACKENING; (3) IT HAS RIPENED TO THE POINT OF GIVING TO A SLIGHT PRESSURE BUT IS NOT SO RIPE THAT THE PIT HAS COME LOOSE AND RATTLES WHEN YOU SHAKE IT. SUCH AN AVOCADO NEEDS ONLY A SQUIRT OF LIME AND A PINCH EACH OF MINCED ONION, FRESH CHILI, AND CILANTRO TO ELEVATE THE FRUIT INTO A DISH.

3 ripe medium avocados, preferably Hass

1½ tablespoons minced onion

1 teaspoon minced jalapeño or serrano chili

1 tablespoon chopped cilantro leaves

1½ tablespoons fresh lime juice

½ teaspoon salt

Cut the avocados in half and remove the pits. Scoop the pulp into a bowl and add the onion, jalapeño, cilantro, lime juice, and salt. Mash with a fork to make a somewhat smooth but still chunky mixture. Use right away or within a few hours.

NOTE: If you are making the guacamole in advance, you can preserve its freshness for up to several hours by tucking the pits into the center of the mixture and covering with plastic wrap, patted down on the surface to keep out air. Refrigerate until ready to use, for up to several hours but not overnight. Remove the plastic wrap and the pits and remix before serving.

TOASTED PUMPKIN SEEDS

✺

MAKES 2 CUPS

PUMPKIN SEEDS ARE CULLED FROM MORE THAN JUST PUMPKINS. THEY CAN ALSO BE THE SEEDS OF MANY KINDS OF LARGE WINTER SQUASHES. IN MEXICO THEY'RE CALLED **PEPITAS**, ARE USUALLY GREEN, AND SHOW UP IN MANY WAYS—ENVELOPED IN A CANDY BRITTLE; GROUND INTO **MOLE** SAUCES; ROASTED WHOLE, SALTED, AND CHILIED, TO CARRY AWAY FOR A STREET SNACK; OR AS A SMALL DISH OF TOASTED SEEDS SET ON THE TABLE TO SPRINKLE ON THIS AND THAT THROUGHOUT THE MEAL.

Spread the pumpkin seeds in an ungreased, large, heavy skillet. Stir over medium heat until the seeds are brown in spots and some are starting to pop, about 3 minutes, or spread the seeds on a plate and microwave, uncovered, on high for 3 minutes. While still warm, sprinkle the seeds lightly with salt. Cool and use right away or store in an airtight container for up to 1 week.

NOTE: You can make your own *pepitas,* golden rather than green, from seeds you save from a pumpkin or other winter squash and roast yourself. Scoop out the seeds from the pumpkin or squash and remove the stringy fibers. Rinse the seeds, pat them dry, and spread in a single layer on a baking sheet or microwave plate. Place in a 325 degree F. oven for 30 minutes or microwave, uncovered, on high for 5 minutes. Add ½ teaspoon peanut oil, stir to coat the seeds, and continue roasting for 30 minutes more, or microwave for 5 minutes more, until golden and crunchy. Sprinkle with salt, if desired, and enjoy when cool enough to eat or store in an airtight container for up to several weeks.

*2 cups unsalted roasted pumpkin seeds
(10 ounces)*
Salt to taste

MEXICAN CRUDITÉS

❉

RAW GARNISHES FOR THE MEXICAN TABLE

SERVES 4

I T'S CURIOUS THERE'S NO SPANISH EQUIVALENT FOR THE DESCRIPTIVE FRENCH TERM "CRUDITÉS," SINCE IN MEXICAN DINING ONE IS ALWAYS TREATED TO A SELECTION OF THEM. LIKE OUR SALT AND PEPPER, FINELY CUT RAW OR BRIEFLY WILTED VEGETABLES ARE PART OF THE MEXICAN TABLE SETTING. THEY ARE OFFERED EITHER IN SMALL INDIVIDUAL BOWLS OR ARRANGED IN SMALL PILES ON THE SIDE OF THE MAIN DISH. THEY PROVIDE A CRISP HIGHLIGHT FOR SOUP, RICE, BEANS, TACOS, TAMALES, ENCHILADAS, AND SO ON. I LIKE TO SET OUT A MIXED PLATTER OF THE FOLLOWING USUAL AND UNUSUAL ONES. THE ARRAY IS ENOUGH TO EMBELLISH THE PLATES OF FOUR DINERS.

WILTED RED ONIONS

❉

½ cup Fruit Vinegar (page 12) or cider vinegar

½ tablespoon sugar

½ jalapeño chili, stemmed and minced

1 medium red onion, halved and thinly sliced

Place the vinegar and sugar in a small saucepan and bring to a boil. Add the jalapeño and onion, stir, and transfer to a serving bowl. Set aside to marinate for 30 minutes or so before using. Can be refrigerated for up to several days.

DRESSED CILANTRO

❉

1 cup cilantro leaves and sprigs, tender parts only

½ teaspoon Fruit Vinegar (page 12) or cider vinegar

⅛ teaspoon salt

½ teaspoon olive oil (optional)

Place the cilantro, vinegar, salt, and olive oil, if using, in a small bowl and toss together. Serve right away.

NOTE: If you do not care for the taste of cilantro, substitute fresh Italian (flat-leaf) parsley leaves.

RADISHES

Wash the radishes and trim off the wilted tops, leaving the small leaves intact. Serve as is or cut the radishes into "roses" and serve the tender leaves on the side.

12 radishes

SHREDDED CABBAGE OR LETTUCE

I always include some very thinly shredded green cabbage or iceberg lettuce on my Mexican crudités plate. Despite the bad press iceberg lettuce receives these days and any disaffection you might have for coarse, stiff pieces of cabbage, when finely cut, these leaves provide a moist, green crunch that is irreplaceable and completes the meal.

Toss the cabbage or lettuce with the salt. Serve right away or set aside at room temperature for up to 2 hours.

¼ medium head green cabbage or iceberg lettuce, cored and very thinly shredded
¼ teaspoon salt

LIMES

In Mexico, almost anywhere you sit down to dine, limes appear, if not on a separate dish of their own, as a slice or two or three on the main plate. Lime complements a Mexican plate perfectly, adding a soft-sour accent that is freshly acetic but not too sharp.

Place the lime wedges on a pretty dish and set on the table.

3 limes, cut into 6 wedges each

FRESH TOMATO SALSA

✺

IN SOUTH-OF-THE-BORDER CUISINE, SOME VERSION OF FRESH TOMATO SALSA IS ALMOST AS USUAL A TABLE SETTING AS SALT AND PEPPER. YOU FIND IT AS **SALSA FRESCA, SALSA CRUDA, SALSA MEXICANA,** AND IN TEXAS, AS **PICO DE GALLO.** SOMETIMES IT'S JUST CALLED "SALSA." ALL THE NAMES AMOUNT TO THE SAME THING—A TONGUE-TINGLING, SPICY, COOLING, AND REFRESHING TOMATO AND CHILI RELISH LACED WITH ONION AND CILANTRO. AS WITH THE NAMES, THE INGREDIENTS VARY FROM PLACE TO PLACE. THE VEGETABLES ARE MORE OR LESS CHOPPED; A LITTLE SUGAR OR TOMATO PASTE IS INCLUDED IF THE TOMATOES NEED SWEETENING OR THICKENING; SOMETIMES GARLIC IS ADDED IF THE COOK LIKES IT. IN THE YUCATAN, RADISH IS TRADITIONAL, ALONG WITH, PERHAPS, SOME MINCED CABBAGE. I ALWAYS ADD THE RADISH, A FILLIP I LEARNED FROM MY FRIEND AND PARTNER, SUSANNA HOFFMAN, WHO LEARNED IT FROM HER FRIEND TERRY VALDEZ, OF MEXICAN-AMERICAN ORIGIN, AND IT SEEMS TO MAKE THE SAUCE SPECIAL. I ADD MORE CHILIES THAN USUAL BECAUSE AFTER A CERTAIN POINT, ABOUT TWO OR THREE CHILIES, THE SALSA DOESN'T BECOME PARTICULARLY HOTTER, AND I ENJOY THE EXTRA CRUNCH. THE IDEA IS TO HAVE THE SALSA SALADY AND CRISP. THIS CAN BE ACCOMPLISHED EASILY AND QUICKLY IN A FOOD PROCESSOR USING THE PULSE CONTROL TO AVOID MASHING OR PUREEING THE ELEMENTS. IF YOU DON'T HAVE SUCH A MACHINE—OR IF YOU PREFER THE ZEN OF CHOPPING VEGETA-BLES—IT DOESN'T TAKE MUCH LONGER TO CUT THE VEGETABLES BY HAND.

4 to 6 small fresh chilies, such as
    jalapeños, serranos, güeros, or a
    mixture, stemmed (about 2 ounces)

½ small onion

2 medium tomatoes (½ pound)

3 large radishes, trimmed

1 cup cilantro leaves

1 garlic clove (optional)

¼ teaspoon salt

1 tablespoon tomato paste (optional)

¼ to ½ cup water, as needed, depending
    on how juicy the tomatoes are

Using a food processor or chef's knife, chop the chilies, onion, tomatoes, radishes, cilantro, and garlic, if using, into $1/16$- to $1/8$-inch pieces. Transfer the vegetables to a medium bowl and stir in the salt, tomato paste, if using, and enough water to make a moist, saucy mixture. Use right away or cover and refrigerate for up to 3 days.

SALSA RANCHERA

✸

MAKES 2 CUPS

SALSA RANCHERA COMES TO THE TABLE, NOT FOR PREMEAL DIPPING, BUT FOR SAUCING COOKED DISHES. LIKE A CHUNKY KETCHUP, AKIN TO BOTTLED TOMATO-CHILI RELISHES, IT'S AS ALL-PURPOSE AS THOSE FAMILIAR TABLE CONDIMENTS—GOOD FOR TACOS, **HUEVOS RANCHEROS**, FRIED POTATOES, OR HAMBURGERS!

Heat the oil in a heavy skillet over medium-high heat. Add all the ingredients and cook over medium heat, stirring occasionally, until the tomatoes and onions are soft, about 15 minutes. Use right away or cover and refrigerate for up to 10 days.

1 tablespoon olive or peanut oil

4 medium tomatoes, peeled and seeded (page 14), finely chopped, juices reserved (1 pound)

1 small onion, finely chopped

1 garlic clove, finely chopped

2 jalapeño chilies, stemmed and finely chopped

½ teaspoon dried oregano

¼ teaspoon salt

GREEN SAUCES FOR THE TABLE

✺

GREEN SAUCES, OR **SALSAS VERDES**, LIKE THEIR RED COUSINS, ARE A STANDARD TABLE SAUCE THROUGHOUT MEXICO. THEY ESTABLISH THE WELCOMING TONE AND BECKON THE DINER: TORTILLA CHIPS PROVIDED AND NO WAITING REQUIRED. ALSO LIKE RED TABLE SAUCES, GREEN SAUCES COME IN MANY GUISES. SOME ARE COOKED, SOME ARE UNCOOKED, AND SOME STRADDLE THE FENCE WITH BOTH COOKED AND UNCOOKED ELEMENTS. THE BASIC INGREDIENTS—TOMATILLOS, SMALL GREEN CHILIES, AND CILANTRO—REMAIN THE SAME. THE TOMATILLOS ARE OFTEN BLANCHED FIRST TO SOFTEN BOTH THEIR TEXTURE AND THEIR FLAVOR; SOMETIMES RAW OR BLANCHED ONION OR GARLIC, OR BOTH, ARE ADDED. FOLLOWING ARE TWO OF MY FAVORITE RECIPES. IN THE UNCOOKED (**CRUDA**) VERSION, I OMIT ONION AND GARLIC, RELYING ON A SIMPLE COMBINATION WITH A FEW FRESH ELEMENTS. IN THE COOKED (**COCIDA**) SAUCE, I ADD A LITTLE ONION, BLANCHED ALONG WITH THE TOMATILLOS. BOTH VERSIONS PROVIDE A MOIST RELISH GARNISH THAT SUITS ALMOST ANY PLATE.

FRESH TOMATILLO SALSA

✺

MAKES 2 CUPS

8 to 10 medium tomatillos, husked,
    stemmed, and rinsed (¾ pound), or
    1 (10-ounce) can tomatillos, drained
    (page 14)
2 jalapeño or 4 serrano chilies, stemmed
1 cup cilantro leaves
½ teaspoon salt
⅓ to ½ cup water

Using a food processor or chef's knife, very finely chop the tomatillos, chilies, and cilantro. Transfer to a bowl and stir in the salt, along with enough water to make a wet salad mixture. Use right away or cover and refrigerate for up to 3 days.

COOKED GREEN SALSA

✹

MAKES 2 CUPS

Combine the tomatillos, if using fresh ones, and the onion in a saucepan large enough to hold them in a single layer. Add the water and bring to a boil. Cover the pot and simmer for 5 minutes, or until the tomatillos are soft but still hold their shape. Transfer the tomatillos, onion, and ½ cup of the cooking water to a food processor or food mill. Add the chilies, cilantro, and salt and puree. Cool or chill before using. May be refrigerated for up to 3 days.

NOTE: If you are using canned tomatillos, remember they are already blanched, so you should modify the instructions thus: Drain the tomatillos, reserving 1 cup of the liquid. Set the tomatillos aside and pour the liquid into a saucepan. Add the onion, bring to a boil, and proceed with the recipe.

8 to 10 medium tomatillos, husked,
    stemmed, and rinsed (¾ pound), or
    1 (10-ounce) can tomatillos (see
    Note)
¼ small onion, coarsely chopped
1½ cups water
2 jalapeño or 4 serrano chilies, stemmed
1 cup cilantro leaves
½ teaspoon salt

PIQUANT SAUCE WITH CHIPOTLE CHILIES AND TAMARIND

❋

MAKES 2 CUPS

THE ROASTED, SMOKY FLAVOR OF CHIPOTLE CHILIES CHARACTERIZES ONE OF THE BEST PIQUANT TABLE SAUCES OF THE MEXICAN TABLE, ESPECIALLY IN THE SOUTH-CENTRAL STATES. BASED ON DRIED CHILIES—SOMETIMES ARBOLS, CASCABELS, OR GUAJILLOS, AS WELL AS CHIPOTLES—PUREED WITH TOMATOES OR TOMATILLOS, THE **SALSAS PICANTES** ARE EARTHY, HOT, AND SPICY. YOU CAN USE TOMATOES FOR A SWEETER, REDDER SAUCE; USE TOMATILLOS TO PRODUCE A BROWNER COLOR AND SHARPER FLAVOR. I ADD TAMARIND, A FAVORITE FLAVORING IN LATIN AMERICAN, ASIAN, AND INDIAN COOKING, TO ACCENTUATE THE DUAL NATURE OF THE CHIPOTLE SAUCE, AT THE SAME TIME SMOKY AND FRUITY, SWEET AND TART.

1 tamarind pod, shelled, or walnut-size pinch tamarind pulp (see Note)

½ cup warm water

8 dried or canned chipotle chilies, stemmed

8 to 10 medium tomatillos, stemmed and husked (about ¾ pound), or 2 medium tomatoes (½ pound)

3 garlic cloves, unpeeled

½ teaspoon salt

Soak the tamarind in the water until softened, about 15 minutes. If using fresh tamarind, rub the pulp off the seeds into the water. Discard the seeds.

Heat a heavy ungreased skillet over high heat. If using dried chipotles, place them in the skillet and stir over medium-high heat until lightly toasted all around, about 1 minute. Remove and set aside. Place the tomatillos or tomatoes and garlic in the skillet and char them over medium heat, turning once or twice, until softened and blackened in spots, about 15 minutes. Remove and cool enough to handle. Peel the garlic and tomatillos. If using tomatoes, leave them unpeeled.

Using a food processor or food mill, puree the tamarind pulp and liquid, chilies, garlic, tomatillos or tomatoes, and salt, adding a little extra water if necessary to make a fluid mixture. Use right away or cover and refrigerate for up to 1 week.

NOTE: Fresh tamarind pods and tamarind pulp pressed into a block are both available in Latin American and Asian markets. To use fresh tamarind, open the pods as you would peas and soak in warm water until soft. Remove and discard the seeds and stiff connecting fibers. To use block tamarind pulp, simply pinch off as much as you need and soak to soften. If neither is available, substitute a few sun-dried apricot halves and dried dates. Soak to soften in a mixture of half lemon juice and half water.

SMOKY TOMATO KETCHUP

✺

MAKES 4 CUPS

IS THERE ANYONE WHO DOESN'T LOVE KETCHUP? THOUGH ITS ORIGINS ARE CHINESE, WITH A FISH PASTE BASE, WE THINK OF IT AS OUR OWN, WITH THE NEW WORLD'S OWN FRUIT, THE TOMATO, AS THE BASE. THOUGH BOTTLED VERSIONS ABOUND, MANY QUITE TASTY AS WELL AS CONVENIENT, BUT IN LATE SUMMER, WHEN YOUR BACKYARD VINES ARE HEAVY LADEN, FRUIT DROPPING TO THE GROUND, AND MARKETS ARE STACKED HIGH WITH PILES OF RIPE TOMATOES AT AN IRRESISTIBLE PRICE, YOU MAY BE TEMPTED TO TRY YOUR OWN RENDITION. THIS ONE IS A SLICK COMPOSITE OF MEXICAN AND NORTH AMERICAN SAUCES, A SMOKY AND PIQUANT RANCHERA, LONG-COOKED AND PUREED INTO A SMOOTH KETCHUP. IT KEEPS WELL, SO YOU MIGHT AS WELL MAKE A LARGE BATCH.

Combine all the ingredients in a large, nonreactive pot and bring to a boil over medium heat. Reduce the heat and simmer for 1½ hours, stirring occasionally, until the vegetables are completely soft and the sauce is reduced by a fourth.

Puree the sauce in a food processor or food mill. Strain through a sieve into a clean pot. Bring to a boil over medium-low heat and simmer for 1 hour, or until quite thick and dark brownish red. Chill before using. Can be refrigerated for up to several weeks. Freeze for longer storage.

5 pounds ripe tomatoes, coarsely chopped

1 large onion, finely chopped

1 large poblano chili, stemmed, seeded, and finely chopped

2 jalapeño chilies, stemmed and coarsely chopped

2 dried or canned chipotle chilies, stemmed

½ cup cider vinegar

1 cup (packed) dark brown sugar

1 teaspoon celery seed

1½ teaspoons mustard seed

¼ teaspoon cayenne

1 teaspoon black pepper

1½ teaspoons salt

JÍCAMA AND WATERMELON SALSA

✵

MAKES 2 CUPS

JÍCAMA LOOKS LIKE A DIRT-BROWN TURNIP OR BEET. IN TEXTURE AND TASTE IT RESEMBLES A FRESH WATER CHESTNUT, THOUGH IT'S DRIER AND SWEETER IN TASTE, AND BOTANICALLY THEY'RE NOT RELATED AT ALL. ONCE PECULIAR TO MEXICAN COOKING, JÍCAMA'S SWEET CRUNCH, IF NOT ITS SOMEWHAT UNSIGHTLY APPEARANCE, HAS BECOME WIDELY APPEALING, AND YOU CAN GENERALLY FIND IT IN SUPERMARKETS THESE DAYS. IT HAS A NATURAL AFFINITY TO CITRUS, A FACT WELL KNOWN TO MEXICAN COOKS WHO GENERALLY SERVE IT RAW, SLICED OR DICED AND SPRINKLED WITH LIME JUICE AND CHILI POWDER OR ALONGSIDE ORANGE SLICES AS THEIR KIND OF **PICO DE GALLO** (NOT THE TEXAS TOMATO SALSA VERSION). ONCE, WHEN SEARCHING FOR A REFRESHING WAY TO TONE DOWN A RICH AND SPICY MEAL, IN A MOMENT OF INSPIRATION I TOSSED JÍCAMA WITH SOME EQUALLY MOIST, CRUNCHY, AND SWEET WATERMELON. I GARNISHED THE COMBINATION WITH MINT AND A SPLASH OF LIME JUICE AND NO CHILI AT ALL. **OLE!**— A NEW TAKE ON AN OLD STANDBY WITH EXTRA COOLING EFFECT.

Toss together the jícama, watermelon, scallion, and lime juice in a medium bowl. Set aside to marinate for 15 minutes or so. Mix in the mint and serve while still fresh and crunchy.

1 small or ½ medium jícama, peeled and cut into ⅛-inch dice (½ pound)

½ pound watermelon, peeled and cut into ⅛-inch dice

1 scallion, trimmed and minced

1 tablespoon fresh lime juice

1 tablespoon shredded fresh mint leaves

MELON JALAPEÑO SALSA

FAR FROM THE VALLEYS OF PERSIA WHERE THEY WERE ORIGINALLY CULTIVATED, MELONS ALSO GROW TO PERFUMED EXCELLENCE IN THE AMERICAS. FROM THE DILUVIAL PLAINS OF CALIFORNIA ALL THE WAY SOUTH TO CHILE AND ARGENTINA, THEY ARE AN OLD WORLD INGREDIENT WHOLEHEARTEDLY INCORPORATED INTO NEW WORLD EATING. COUPLED WITH THE BITE OF CHILI, TRIPLED WITH THE FRAGRANCE OF CILANTRO, MELON BECOMES THE STUFF OF A FRESH, NEW SALSA FOR THE MODERN KITCHEN.

1 small or ½ large cantaloupe or honey-
    dew melon, peeled, seeded, and cut
    into ¼-inch dice
1 serrano or ½ jalapeño chili, stemmed
    and minced
2 tablespoons chopped cilantro leaves
1 tablespoon fresh lime juice

Place all the ingredients in a bowl and stir gently to mix. Serve right away or cover and chill. Use the same day.

PAPAYA AND PEANUT SALSA

❋

MAKES ABOUT 2 CUPS

ONCE YOU HAVE THE IDEA OF COMBINING FRUIT INTO A SAVORY MIXTURE, A WORLD OF RELISH POSSIBILITIES OPENS. STARTING WITH DICED FRUIT—PAPAYA, MANGO, GRAPEFRUIT, PINEAPPLE— ADD THE CRUNCH OF A NUT OR SEED—PEANUT, PINE NUT, **PEPITA**. BRIGHTEN THE FLAVORS WITH A TOUCH OF CHILI, AND YOU HAVE A SALSA CONDIMENT TO ACCOMPANY ANY BEAN, RICE, OR VEGETABLE DISH. I LIKE TO COMBINE PAPAYA WITH PEANUTS, GRAPEFRUIT WITH PUMPKIN SEEDS AND SERVE THEM AS A DUO, BUT THESE ARE JUST EXAMPLES OF WHERE YOUR IMAGINATION CAN LEAD YOU.

Place the peanuts, garlic, chili powder, and oil in a heavy skillet or on a microwaveable plate and toss to coat. Stir over medium-high heat or microwave, uncovered, on high for 2 minutes, or until toasted. Transfer the peanuts to a small bowl, add the remaining ingredients, and stir to mix. Cover and chill for 30 minutes before serving.

½ cup salted roasted peanuts, coarsely chopped (3 ounces)

½ teaspoon oil

1 garlic clove, minced or pressed

½ teaspoon pure chili powder

1 ripe but still firm papaya, peeled, seeded, and cut into ⅛-inch dice (1 pound)

½ small poblano chili, stemmed and minced (about 2 tablespoons)

3 tablespoons fresh lime juice

GRAPEFRUIT AND PUMPKIN SEED SALSA

❋

MAKES ABOUT 2 CUPS

With a knife, remove the peel from the grapefruit, cutting through the white membrane all the way to the pulp. Cut the grapefruit into ¼-inch dice and transfer, along with the juices, to a bowl. Add the remaining ingredients and stir to mix. Cover and chill for 30 minutes before serving.

2 medium-large pink grapefruit

⅓ cup Toasted Pumpkin Seeds (page 21)

1 serrano or ½ jalapeño chili, stemmed and minced

1 medium shallot, minced

1 tablespoon chopped cilantro leaves

CORN AND SWEET RED PEPPER SALSA

✹

MAKES 2 CUPS

IT IS FITTING, THOUGH NOT TYPICAL, THAT CORN AND CAPSICUM BE MIXED INTO A SALSALIKE RELISH FOR THE MEXICAN TABLE. THE COMELY MIX — PALE YELLOW KERNELS, TINY SQUARES OF SWEET RED PEPPER, GREEN FLECKS OF MINCED JALAPEÑO — PAYS TRIBUTE TO TWO OF THE NEW WORLD'S GREAT CONTRIBUTIONS TO CUISINE AND SATISFIES ANY CRAVING YOU MAY HAVE FOR A CRUNCHY, FRESH CONDIMENT TO ACCOMPANY YOUR MEAL.

½ cup corn kernels (1 small ear of
    corn)
1 medium red bell pepper, stemmed,
    seeded, and cut into ⅛-inch dice
1 jalapeño chili, stemmed and minced
¼ medium onion, finely chopped
½ cup chopped cilantro leaves
⅛ teaspoon ground cumin
½ teaspoon salt
1 teaspoon tomato paste
½ cup water

Bring a small pot of water to a boil. Drop in the corn. Drain immediately and set aside to cool. When cool, place the corn and the remaining ingredients in a medium bowl and gently stir together. Use right away or cover, chill, and use the same day

ROASTED AND MARINATED CHILI STRIPS

✸

MAKES 2 CUPS

RED BELLS, GREEN BELLS, POBLANO CHILIES, ANAHEIM CHILIES, IT MATTERS NOT. IN MEXICAN COOKING, LARGE PEPPERS ARE CUSTOMARILY ROASTED AND PEELED (PAGE 13). MOST USUALLY, THE PEPPERS ARE SLICED INTO STRIPS, OR **RAJAS,** AND ARE SAUTÉED WITH SOME ONION AND OTHER SEASONING. THE DISH **RAJAS** (PAGE 116) IS USED AS A SIDE GARNISH FOR A MAIN PLATE, NOTABLY FOR THE FAMOUS BEEFSTEAK PLATTER CALLED **CARNE ASADA A LA TAMPIQUENA.** OCCASIONALLY, THE STRIPS, WITHOUT FURTHER COOKING, ARE TOSSED WITH RAW ONION SLICES AND LIGHTLY DRESSED WITH CITRUS AND AN HERB TO MAKE A TABLE CONDIMENT REMINISCENT OF MEDITERRANEAN PREPARATIONS, AS HERE.

Cut the chili peppers lengthwise into ⅛-inch strips and place in a bowl. Add the remaining ingredients and toss to mix. Set aside to marinate for at least 30 minutes before serving or cover and refrigerate for up to 5 days.

6 to 8 large green chilies, such as
    poblanos or Anaheims (1 pound),
    roasted, peeled, and seeded (page 13)
1 small onion, halved and very thinly
    sliced
1 teaspoon chopped fresh oregano leaves
    or ½ teaspoon dried oregano
½ cup fresh lime juice

PICKLED MIXED VEGETABLES

❁

MAKES 2 QUARTS

PICKLING, CALLED **EN ESCABECHE**, IS A FAVORITE WAY OF PREPARING ALL MANNER OF FOOD IN MEXICO, BOTH TO ADD FLAVOR TO OTHERWISE BLAND FOODS LIKE TURKEY AND TO EXTEND FRESHNESS IN PERISHABLE FOODS, FISH FOR EXAMPLE. IN THE CASE OF VEGETABLES, PREPARING THEM **EN ESCABECHE** ALLOWS THEM TO BE "PUT BY" IN THE REFRIGERATOR FOR UP TO SEVERAL WEEKS TO HAVE ON HAND ANY TIME YOU'D LIKE A SAVORY SNACK. TRADITIONALLY, THE VEGETABLES ARE A SELECTION OF ONION, GARLIC, CAULIFLOWER, GREEN BEANS, CABBAGE, CACTUS PADS, CORN, GREEN TOMATO, TOMATILLO, CARROT, AND JALAPEÑO OR SERRANO CHILIES, BUT YOU CAN CHOOSE AND MIX AS YOU LIKE AND AS THE SEASON DICTATES. THE PICKLING MEDIUM IS ALWAYS A MILD, FRUITY VINEGAR, LIGHTLY SALTED, WELL HERBED, AND OF COURSE, SPICED WITH FRESH CHILIES. FOLLOWING ARE TWO OF MY FAVORITE, FAIRLY TYPICAL, COMBINATIONS.

¼ cup olive oil

1 medium onion, cut into ¼-inch wedges

8 garlic cloves, peeled and halved

6 small fresh chilies, preferably red

4 cups Fruit Vinegar (page 12) or
    cider vinegar

1 cup water

1 tablespoon fresh marjoram leaves or
    1½ teaspoons dried marjoram

2 large bay leaves

1 tablespoon salt

1 teaspoon black peppercorns, cracked

½ small cauliflower, cored and cut into
    florets (½ pound)

½ pound green beans, whole if small or
    cut into 2-inch lengths if large

2 medium zucchini, trimmed and cut
    into ¼-inch rounds

Heat the oil in a large nonreactive pot or saucepan over medium-high heat. Add the onion, garlic, and chilies and stir over medium heat until the vegetables wilt slightly, about 3 minutes. Add the vinegar, water, marjoram, bay leaves, salt, and peppercorns. Bring to a boil, reduce the heat, and simmer for 3 minutes more.

Place the cauliflower, green beans, and zucchini in a 2-quart glass or heavy plastic container. Carefully transfer the ingredients from the pot to the container. Let cool completely. Cover and refrigerate overnight before serving. Will keep for up to several months in the refrigerator.

PICKLED CARROTS AND JALAPEÑOS

❁

MAKES 5 CUPS

CANS OF PICKLED JALAPEÑO CHILIES AND CARROTS, AVAILABLE EVEN IN HUMBLE GROCERY STORES, TESTIFY TO THE POPULARITY OF THE MEXICAN WAY WITH PICKLING VEGETABLES. THE TINS CONTAIN MORE OF THE GREEN THAN THE ORANGE, IT'S TRUE, BUT IF YOU VISIT A MEXICAN CANTINA YOU MIGHT WELL FIND ON THE TABLE A SMALL BOWL OF MOSTLY CARROTS WITH A FEW JALAPEÑO ROUNDS TO HEAT THEM UP. AT HOME, I EVEN THE MEASURE BETWEEN THE CARROTS AND CHILIES AND ADD LIME JUICE AND A PINCH OF CARAWAY. USE THESE AS YOU WOULD ANY PICKLE, SALSA, OR RELISH.

2 cups Fruit Vinegar (page 12) or cider vinegar

¼ cup fresh lime juice

¼ cup olive oil

1 cup water

½ tablespoon fresh marjoram leaves or 1 teaspoon dried marjoram

1 large bay leaf

1 teaspoon caraway seeds

½ tablespoon salt

1 teaspoon cracked black pepper

4 to 5 carrots, scraped and cut diagonally into ¼-inch ovals (1 pound)

12 to 15 jalapeño chilies, pricked with a knife to make a small slit in each (½ pound)

1 medium onion, cut into ¼-inch wedges, layers separated

6 garlic cloves, peeled and halved

Place the vinegar, lime juice, oil, water, marjoram, bay leaf, caraway seeds, salt, and pepper in a large nonreactive pot. Bring to a boil over high heat. Add the carrots, jalapeños, onion, and garlic. Bring to a boil, reduce the heat, and simmer until the vegetables start to wilt, about 2 minutes. Remove from the heat and cool completely, at least 45 minutes.

Transfer the cooled vegetables and liquid to a glass or heavy plastic container, cover, and refrigerate overnight before serving. Will keep, refrigerated, for up to several weeks.

HOMEMADE THICKENED CREAM

✺

MAKES 2 CUPS

THE SPANISH INTRODUCED CATTLE TO MEXICO, AND BOVINE HUSBANDRY HAS FLOURISHED THERE EVER SINCE, BOTH FOR BEEF AND DAIRY PURPOSES. THE MEXICAN LOVE OF SUCH PRODUCTS IS REFLECTED IN ALL THEIR COOKING. FROM SNACKS TO THE MAIN MEAL, BEEF IS A PRIME INGREDIENT. ON THE DAIRY SIDE, CANS, BOTTLES, AND CANDIES OF **LECHE** LINE THE SHELVES OF MEXICAN MARKETS. THE PLETHORA OF REGIONAL CHEESES MAKES YOU WONDER HOW PEOPLE GOT ALONG BEFORE COW'S MILK. AND THEN THERE'S CREAM. IN MEXICO, THE CREAM COMES RICH, THICK, AND SLIGHTLY TANGY. UNLIKE THE SOUR CREAM WE'VE LEARNED TO SUBSTITUTE IN MEXICAN DISHES, IT'S EARTHY — ALMOST GRASSY — IN TASTE. YOU CAN CREATE SOMETHING SIMILAR BY MIXING A BIT OF BUTTERMILK INTO ORDINARY CREAM TO PRODUCE THE RIGHT THICKNESS AND TYPICAL EVER-SO-MILDLY-TART FLAVOR THAT DOESN'T RELINQUISH ANY SWEETNESS.

Stir the cream and buttermilk together in a glass or heavy plastic container. Cover and set aside at room temperature until well thickened, 12 to 36 hours, depending on the temperature and degree of pasteurization of the cream. Use right away or store in the refrigerator for up to 10 days.

1½ cups heavy cream
2 teaspoons buttermilk

chapter two

TORTILLA
CUISINE

STREET FOOD AND
LIGHT MEALS

✺

THE PRODUCTION, PREPARATION, CONSUMPTION, AND ENJOYMENT OF FOOD MAKE UP A MAJOR SEG-
MENT OF COMMERCE AND DAILY LIFE IN MEXICO. In every village, town, and city, food is everywhere. Eating is not reserved for a certain two or three times a day at table. It is part of the public domain. From handbaskets to stands, stalls, cafes, and restaurants, food treats are proffered at every hour on every corner. Snack in hand, people walk along the street, lean on a counter, rest on a bench in the town square, pull up a chair in a *botanas* (snack and small plate) bar.

Almost always a tortilla is involved. From both the Spanish and native Indian languages and culinary traditions comes a poetic bouquet of names. After *tortillas de maiz, tortillas de harina,* tostadas, and other familiar ones, you have *totopos, panuchos, sopes, gorditas, tortas, uchepos,* and more.

Whether corn or flour, large or minuscule, thick or thin, doughy or crepey, filled or unfilled—the divergent range of shapes and textures is wonderful—these unleavened flat cakes enfold or accompany almost every food. Tortillas appear as wrappers, holders, edible plates, table bread. You can fill, loosely roll, and bake them for enchiladas; fill, tightly roll, and fry them for flautas; make envelope packages stuffed with any concoction you desire and deep-fry or steam them for chimichangas or burritos; or quickly crisp them and add toppings for tostadas. Along with other corn-flour preparations like tamales and wheat-flour treats like empanadas, tortillas make up the savory snacks and light meals of Mexican cooking.

CORN TORTILLAS

✺

MAKES 18 6- TO 7-INCH TORTILLAS

WE KNOW BOTH CORN AND FLOUR TORTILLAS, BUT THE ORIGINAL ONES WERE OF THE NATIVE CORN ONLY, AND EXCEPT IN NORTHERN MEXICO, CORN TORTILLAS REMAIN THE NORM AND THE STAPLE. AS WITH BREADS AROUND THE WORLD, THE MAKING OF CORN TORTILLAS, THOUGH A SOMEWHAT PRECISE PROCESS, IS NOT COMPLICATED. TODAY, WE HAVE THE ADVANTAGE OF PURCHASING EXCELLENT-QUALITY CORN TORTILLAS, BUT NONE RIVALS THE BEST HAND-PATTED ONES FRESH OFF THE BRAZIER ON A CERTAIN STREET CORNER IN MEXICO, YOU-CAN'T-QUITE-REMEMBER-WHERE, OR, PERHAPS, THOSE YOU TAKE A NOTION TO MAKE YOURSELF. SO I OFFER A SIMPLE RECIPE FOR HOMEMADE CORN TORTILLAS USING EASY-TO-MIX **MASA HARINA**. WHEN YOU MAKE YOUR OWN, YOU CAN PAT OR PRESS THE TORTILLAS AS THEY DO IN MEXICO INTO ANY SHAPE AND SIZE TO SUIT YOURSELF.

Place the *masa harina* and salt in a large bowl. Add the water and mix with your hands to make a dough that comes together in a soft ball. Continue mixing and kneading until the dough is elastic enough to hold together without cracking, about 3 minutes. If using right away, divide the dough into 18 equal portions and cover with plastic wrap or a damp towel. If making in advance to use later, wrap the whole ball in plastic wrap and refrigerate for up to 1 day and divide later.

To form the tortillas, place a portion of dough between 2 pieces of plastic wrap. Press with a tortilla press or roll out with a rolling pin into a circle 6- to 7-inches in diameter. Use your fingers to smooth any raggedy edges. Continue with the remaining portions until the dough is used up.

To cook the tortillas, heat a heavy skillet, griddle, or *comal* over high heat until it begins to smoke. Peel the plastic wrap off a tortilla and place the tortilla in the pan. Reduce the heat to medium-high and cook for 30 seconds. Turn and cook on the other side for 1 minute. Turn again, and cook until the tortilla puffs a bit but is still pliable, not crisp, about 30 seconds more. Remove and continue until all the tortillas are cooked. Serve soon. Corn tortillas are best freshly made.

4 cups masa harina *(page 11)*
½ teaspoon salt
2½ cups hot but not boiling water

FLOUR TORTILLAS

✺

MAKES 12 8-INCH TORTILLAS

FLOUR TORTILLAS—**TORTILLAS DE HARINA**—MADE A LATE APPEARANCE ON THE MEXICAN TABLE, AFTER THE SPANISH BROUGHT WHEAT TO MEXICO IN THE SIXTEENTH CENTURY. THOUGH WHEAT-FLOUR BREADS AND SWEETS ARE NOW COMMON THROUGHOUT MEXICO, FLOUR TORTILLAS BECAME THE BREAD STAPLE IN THE NORTHERN STATES ONLY. THEY ARE TRADITIONALLY MADE WITH LARD, BUT FOR HEALTH REASONS, MODERN COOKS AND MANY TORTILLA FACTORIES NOW HAVE SWITCHED TO VEGETABLE SHORTENING OR VEGETABLE OIL, WITH NO LOSS OF GOOD RESULTS IN MY OPINION. RATHER THAN PATTED OR PRESSED, FLOUR TORTILLAS ARE ROLLED OUT, THEN STRETCHED INTO CIRCLES RANGING FROM THREE TO TWENTY INCHES, DEPENDING ON HOW THEY ARE TO BE USED. FOR THE HOME COOK INEXPERIENCED IN THE ART OF SPINNING WIDER DIAMETERS OUT OF THE DOUGH, LIKE AN ACE PIZZA TOSSER, EIGHT INCHES IS A MANAGEABLE SIZE.

3 cups unbleached all-purpose flour

1 teaspoon salt

⅓ cup vegetable shortening or oil

1 cup warm but not boiling water

Combine the flour, salt, and shortening in a large bowl and mix together until crumbly, as for pie dough. Add the water and mix until you can gather the dough into a ball. Transfer the dough to a lightly floured surface and knead until smooth and elastic, about 5 minutes. Cover with plastic wrap and set aside to rest in a warm place for at least 30 minutes or up to 2 hours.

To form the tortillas, divide the dough into 12 equal portions. Roll each portion between the palms of your hands to make a ball. On a lightly floured surface, roll out each ball into an 8-inch circle. Layer the circles between sheets of plastic wrap as you go.

To cook the tortillas, heat a heavy skillet, griddle, or *comal* over high heat until beginning to smoke. Place a tortilla in the pan and cook for 30 seconds. Turn and cook on the other side until slightly puffed and speckled brown on the underside but still soft enough to fold, about 30 seconds. Remove and continue until all the tortillas are cooked, stacking them as you go. Serve right away or cool, wrap in plastic wrap, and refrigerate for up to 3 days.

TORTILLA CHIPS

✸

MAKES 36 CHIPS

DON'T TOSS THOSE STALE TORTILLAS! NOT ONLY ARE THEY CALLED FOR IN CERTAIN CLASSIC DISHES SUCH AS CHILAQUILES (PAGE 59) AND TORTILLA SOUP (PAGE 70), THEY'RE EASILY TRANSFORMED INTO TORTILLA CHIPS. WHETHER CORN OR FLOUR, WITH A FEW SWIFT SWIPES OF THE KNIFE YOU CAN CUT THEM INTO WEDGES, TOAST OR FRY THEM, AND MAKE **TOSTADITAS** FOR DIPPING, CRUMBLING, GARNISHING, SNACKING.

6 corn or flour tortillas

Oil for frying (optional)

Salt, to taste

Stack the tortillas and slice through the stack to make 6 wedge cuts.

To cook without oil, preheat the oven to 400 degrees F. Separate the tortilla wedges and arrange them, without overlapping, on a baking sheet. Place in the oven and bake for 5 minutes. Turn and bake 5 minutes more, until toasted and crisp.

To fry, pour oil into a heavy skillet to a depth of ¼ inch. Heat over high heat until the oil sizzles when you dip in a corner of a tortilla wedge. Place as many wedges as will fit without overlapping into the oil and fry until they begin to puff, about 1 minute. Turn with a spatula or slotted spoon and fry until crisp, about 1½ minutes more, adjusting the heat as you go to keep the pieces from burning. Remove to paper towels to drain. Continue until all the wedges are crisped.

Salt to taste and serve right away or cool and store in an airtight container for up to 2 weeks.

CHILES CON QUESO

✸

SERVES 6

WHEN YOUNG, I THOUGHT OF CHILES CON QUESO AS AN AMERICAN DISH. MY MOTHER, WITH HER SIGNATURE TEX-MEX FLAIR, RITUALLY PREPARED IT FOR LARGE GATHERINGS. LATER, I FOUND OUT THE DISH HAD BEEN IMPORTED TO THE SOUTHWESTERN UNITED STATES BY MIGRANT WORKERS AND TOURISTS BACK FROM NORTHERN MEXICO AND THUS EVENTUALLY TO OUR HOUSEHOLD. MORE SVELTE AND LESS SPICY THAN THE MELTED CHEESE-AND-JALAPEÑO RINGS-WITH-CHIPS WE KNOW AND LOVE AS NACHOS, CHILES CON QUESO WITH SOFT **ASADERO** CHEESE AND MILD ANAHEIM CHILIES FILL THE CHIPS-AND-DIP BILL IN A MORE SOPHISTICATED, PARTY-FOOD WAY.

4 tablespoons (½ stick) butter

1 large onion, finely chopped

6 fresh Anaheim chilies, roasted, peeled, and seeded (page 13), or canned whole green chilies

1 large tomato, peeled and seeded, (page 14), and cut into ¼-inch dice

1 pound grated queso asadero, Monterey Jack, or farmer's cheese, or cream cheese

¾ cup Homemade Thickened Cream (page 41), half-and-half, or sour cream thinned with 1½ tablespoons heavy cream

Salt and pepper, to taste

Fresh corn tortillas, warmed, or tortilla chips

Melt the butter in a large skillet. Add the onion and cook over medium heat until slightly wilted but not browned, about 5 minutes. Add the chilies and tomato and simmer until the vegetables are soft, about 10 minutes. Add the cheese and cream and stir over medium-low heat until the cheese melts and the mixture is smooth, about 2 to 3 minutes. Season with salt and pepper to taste and serve right away, accompanied by warm tortillas or tortilla chips.

QUESADILLAS

❀

SERVES 2

BREAD AND CHEESE TOGETHER MAKE UP ONE OF THE WORLD'S ESSENTIAL AND MOST BELOVED QUICK LUNCH, SNACK FOODS. IN MEXICO AND POINTS NORTH ALONG THE GULF AND PACIFIC COAST STATES OF THE UNITED STATES, THE COMBINATION TURNS UP AS QUESADILLAS. THE "BREAD" MAY BE A DOUGHLIKE **MASA** CAKE, A WHEAT-FLOUR TURNOVER, A CORN TORTILLA, OR MOST USUALLY, A FLOUR TORTILLA. LIKE SIMILAR FOODS AROUND THE WORLD, A QUESADILLA IS MEANT TO STAVE HUNGER ON THE SPOT. THE COOK'S CREATIVITY CAN TRANSFORM THE SIMPLE INTO THE SUBLIME. QUESADILLAS CAN BE FILLED WITH A BIT OR TWO OF POTATO AND SOME CHILI STRIPS, SLICED TOMATOES, DICED ONION, MUSHROOMS, SQUASH BLOSSOMS, AND SO ON AS THE IMAGINATION GOES. THE UNCOMPLICATED VERSION, JUST MELTED CHEESE ON A TORTILLA WITH A DOLLOP OF SALSA, PERHAPS REIGNS AS THE MOST ELEGANT. BUT THEN, WHO CAN RESIST A FEW ADDITIONAL FLOURISHES?

2 cups grated semisoft cheese, such as
    Monterey Jack, Gouda, provolone,
    Muenster, cheddar, farmer's cheese, or
    queso asadero (6 ounces)
2 flour or 4 corn tortillas
Oil for frying (optional)

Optional Ingredients
2 jalapeño chilies, stemmed and sliced
2 medium tomatillos, husked, rinsed,
    and sliced into thin rounds
2 scallions, trimmed and minced, or 2
    tablespoons minced red or white onion
4 tablespoons Fresh Tomato Salsa
    (page 24)

Optional Toppings
1 cup thinly shredded lettuce or cabbage
¼ cup Dressed Cilantro (page 22)
4 grilled baby onions (page 125)

Spread the cheese over the tortillas. Add as many optional ingredients as you are using.

To fry the quesadillas, lightly grease a heavy skillet with oil and heat until smoking. Place a tortilla in the skillet and cook over medium-high heat until the cheese begins to melt, about 1 minute. Fold the tortilla in half. Cook until lightly browned on each side, about 1 minute altogether. Continue until all the tortillas are cooked.

To cook without oil, preheat the oven to 400 degrees F. Place the tortillas without folding on a baking sheet and bake until the cheese melts, about 5 minutes.

Place as many optional toppings as you are using over the cheese. If cooked in the oven, fold in half. Serve right away while still warm and tender.

NOTE: Though quesadillas are meant to be handheld, you can offer them with a salad for lunch or a light supper entree.

NACHOS

✲

FOR 1 PLATE

FOR A LESS FANCY, MORE BALLPARK, YET MOST SATISFYING RENDITION OF CHIPS, CHILIES, AND CHEESE, YOU CAN PUT YOUR MICROWAVE TO GOOD USE AND TURN OUT NACHOS IN NO TIME. THEY ARE ONE OF THE BEST ANY-TIME-OF-DAY SNACKS THERE IS.

½ recipe Tortilla Chips (page 49) or
    18 purchased tortilla chips
2 cups grated semisoft cheese, such as
    cheddar, Monterey Jack, Gouda,
    Muenster, or a mixture (6 ounces)
6 pickled jalapeño chilies, canned or
    homemade, cut into ⅛-inch rounds,
    stems discarded (see Note)

Mound the chips on a microwave-safe plate. Sprinkle the cheese over the chips and arrange the jalapeño slices on top. Microwave, uncovered, on high for 1½ minutes, or until the cheese is melted. Serve right away.

NOTE: For homemade pickled jalapeños, see the recipe for Pickled Carrots and Jalapeños (page 40).

GREEN ENCHILADAS IN MOLE VERDE

SERVES 4 TO 6

THE TORTILLAS FOR GREEN ENCHILADAS, UNLIKE THOSE FOR THE RED, ARE SOFTENED IN OIL BEFORE THEY ARE DIPPED IN SAUCE AND FILLED. THE SAUCE I USE HERE, A NUTTY AND DEEPLY FLAVORED MOLE VERDE, GREEN WITH TOMATILLOS, CHILIES, AND FRESH HERBS, IS BASED SIMPLY ON PUMPKIN SEEDS. IT MAKES A SPLENDID COVERING FOR ENCHILADAS.

Put the mole verde in a medium saucepan and set it over low heat to keep warm without boiling.

Heat 1 tablespoon of the oil in a heavy skillet. Add a tortilla and fry over medium-high heat until soft and pliable but not crisp, about 1 minute.

Dip the tortilla into the sauce to coat both sides. Spread 1 tablespoon of the grated cheese in the center and roll up to make a loose tube about ¾ inch in diameter. Set it, seam side down, on a serving platter and continue, adding more oil to the skillet as necessary, until all the tortillas are softened, filled, and rolled.

Pour the remaining sauce over the enchiladas. Drizzle with the cream, garnish with the onion, and serve right away.

2 cups Mole Verde (recipe follows)

¼ cup vegetable oil

12 corn tortillas

1 cup grated semisoft cheese, such as Monterey Jack, farmer's cheese, or queso fresco (3 ounces)

1 cup Homemade Thickened Cream (page 41) or sour cream, thinned with 2 tablespoons heavy cream, at room temperature

½ medium red or white onion, very thinly sliced

MOLE VERDE

MAKES 2 CUPS

Place the tomatillos, onion, garlic, and water in a small saucepan. Bring to a boil, then cover and simmer for 5 minutes, or until the vegetables soften.

Place the pumpkin seeds and 2 tablespoons of the cooking liquid in a food processor and chop fine. Add the chilies, lettuce, cilantro, salt, and the remaining cooking water and puree as fine as possible.

Heat the oil in a skillet over high heat. Add the pureed mixture and stir over medium-high heat until thickened and no longer bright green, about 5 minutes. Use right away or cool, cover, and refrigerate overnight. Reheat before using.

3 tomatillos, husked, stemmed, and rinsed

½ small onion, coarsely chopped

1 large garlic clove, coarsely chopped

½ cup water

⅓ cup Toasted Pumpkin Seeds (page 21)

4 medium poblano chilies, roasted, peeled, and seeded (page 13)

1 large leaf romaine lettuce, shredded

¼ cup cilantro leaves

½ teaspoon salt

1 tablespoon peanut oil

RED ENCHILADAS

✸

SERVES 4 TO 6

WHEN IT COMES TO ENCHILADAS, OPINIONS RUN STRONG AS TO WHICH IS BETTER, RED OR GREEN. RED ENCHILADASUSUALLY ENCASE A CHEESE OR MEAT FILLING AND ARE BLANKETED IN A RED SAUCE WITH A SPRINKLE OF ONION ON TOP. GREEN ENCHILADAS USUALLY HAVE A CHICKEN FILLING AND A GREEN SAUCE WITH THICKENED CREAM OR SOUR CREAM FOR TOPPING. BEYOND THEIR DIFFERENCES, ENCHILADAS ARE THE SAME AT HEART: SAUCED, SOFTENED TORTILLAS, FILLED, ROLLED, GARNISHED, AND SERVED UP. WHETHER YOU PREFER THE RED OR THE GREEN, THERE'S NO REASON TO LIMIT YOURSELF TO THE STANDARD VERSIONS. I LIKE TWO SOMEWHAT OUT-OF-THE-ORDINARY VEGETARIAN INNOVATIONS, BOTH EASY TO PREPARE.

3 cups Red Enchilada Sauce
(recipe follows)
¼ cup vegetable oil
12 corn tortillas
1 cup grated semisoft cheese, such as
Monterey Jack, farmer's cheese, or
queso fresco (3 ounces)
½ cup crumbled feta or cotija cheese
(2 ounces)
½ cup salted, roasted peanuts, finely
chopped
1 cup Dressed Cilantro (page 22)

Place the sauce in a medium saucepan and set over very low heat to keep warm as you proceed with the recipe.

Heat 1 tablespoon of the oil in a heavy skillet over high heat. Dip a tortilla in the sauce, coating it on both sides. Place the coated tortilla in the skillet and fry over medium-high heat on both sides to soften without crisping, about 1 minute.

Spread 1 tablespoon of the grated cheese in the center of the tortilla, roll up, then place, seam side down, on a serving platter. Continue with the remaining tortillas, adding more oil to the skillet as necessary, until all are softened, filled, and rolled.

Pour the remaining sauce over the enchiladas. Sprinkle the crumbled cheese and peanuts over the top, garnish with the cilantro sprigs, and serve right away.

NOTE: Red or green, enchiladas are normally not baked. But for large gatherings you can put together the enchiladas in advance, arrange them in a single layer in a baking dish, and heat them in a hot oven before serving.

RED ENCHILADA SAUCE

※

MAKES 3 CUPS

Place the chilies, tomatoes, garlic, and water in a medium saucepan and bring to a boil. Reduce the heat, cover, and simmer for 5 minutes, or until the chilies soften. Lift out the tomatoes, let cool enough to handle, and peel them. Set aside the saucepan.

Place the tomatoes, cumin, oregano, salt, and contents of the saucepan in a food processor and puree as smooth as possible.

Transfer the puree to a clean saucepan and keep warm over low heat if using right away or cool, cover, and refrigerate for up to 1 week. Reheat before using.

4 to 6 large ancho chilies, stemmed, torn in half, and seeded (about 2 ounces)

2 small dried red chilies, arbols or japones, stemmed, torn in half, and seeded

3 medium tomatoes (¾ pound)

4 garlic cloves, coarsely chopped

1½ cups water

½ teaspoon ground cumin

½ teaspoon dried oregano

½ teaspoon salt

SIMMERED VEGETABLE TACOS

✸

SERVES 6

WHETHER YOU GET ONE IN HAND OR ON A PLATE, FROM A STREET VENDOR, IN A RESTAURANT, OR AT HOME, THERE IS NOTHING BETTER THAN A TACO. WITHIN THE SUPPLE TORTILLA WRAPPER, THE INDIAN AND SPANISH CULTURES MEET IN A MOST OBLIGING WAY. HERE, I OFFER AN EXEMPLARY FAVORITE, CREATED BY MY FRIEND AND PARTNER SUSANNA HOFFMAN. SHE CONCOCTED IT ON THE SPUR OF THE MOMENT ONE EVENING FOR SOME FRIENDS WHO, INVITED TO DINNER FOR TURKEY TACOS, CALLED JUST BEFORE ARRIVING TO SAY THEY WOULD BE BRINGING A FEW EXTRA FRIENDS ALONG, IF THAT'S OK, AND BY THE WAY, THEY DON'T EAT ANY FLESH. SHE HUSTLED AROUND THE KITCHEN FOR VEGETABLES, AND EVERYONE SO LIKED THE OUTCOME, THE NON–MEAT EATERS FOR WHOM THE DISH WAS TO BE DINNER BARELY GOT THEIR SHARE. WE'VE SERVED SIMMERED VEGETABLE TACOS TO APPLAUSE ON COUNTLESS OCCASIONS SINCE, AND IN A FEW COOKBOOKS BESIDES, PROVING A GOOD TACO SPINS ITSELF INTO GOLD.

2 cups corn kernels (from 4 large ears
   of corn)

5 medium red or white potatoes,
   scrubbed and cut into ¼-inch pieces
   (about 1½ pounds)

1 large onion, cut into ¼-inch dice

3 medium zucchini, trimmed and cut
   into ¼-inch dice (¾ pound)

6 medium tomatoes, coarsely chopped
   into ½-inch pieces (1½ pounds)

1 jalapeño chili, stemmed and minced

1 tablespoon fresh oregano leaves or
   1 teaspoon dried oregano

1½ teaspoons salt

¾ cup white wine

¼ cup coarsely chopped cilantro leaves1

12 warm flour tortillas

1 cup sour cream

Combine the corn, potatoes, onion, zucchini, tomatoes, jalapeño, oregano, salt, and wine in a large nonreactive pot. Set the pot over medium-high heat and cook, stirring once or twice, for 15 minutes, or until the potatoes are done. Stir in the cilantro and remove from the heat. Serve right away, scooped into a warm tortilla and topped with the cream.

CHILAQUILES

※

SERVES 6

CHILAQUILES, A TORTILLA CASSEROLE SUPREME, IS A NATIONAL DISH OF MEXICO. IT VARIES IN THE KIND OF CHILI, THE CHEESE, THE TOMATOES (RED OR GREEN, NONE AT ALL), AND THE SHAPE OF THE TORTILLA PIECES (STRIPS, SQUARES, DIAMONDS). BUT THE UNDERLYING CONCEPT REMAINS THE SAME: NOTHING FANCY; GOOD HOT OR COLD; EAT IT NOW OR HAVE LEFTOVERS (ALL THE BETTER).

Heat the oil in a heavy skillet over high heat until it begins to smoke. Place as many tortilla strips in the pan as will fit without overlapping. Fry over medium-high heat, pressing down on the pieces to cook the tops also, for a few seconds, until barely golden but not crisp. Remove to paper towels to drain. Continue until all the tortillas are fried.

Drain the oil from the skillet, leaving a thin coating, and add the tomatoes, onion, chilies, epazote, water, salt, and pepper. Cook over medium heat until the onions and tomatoes soften, about 8 minutes.

Add the tortilla pieces to the skillet and sprinkle the cheese over the top. Cover and simmer until the cheese melts and the tortillas are soft again but not mushy, about 5 minutes.

Spread the cream over the top, sprinkle with the cilantro, if using, and serve right away.

NOTE: If the tortillas are fresh, not stale, cut them and dry out the pieces in a 200 degree F. oven until no longer pliable but not yet toasted, about 7 minutes.

½ cup vegetable oil

12 stale corn tortillas, cut into 1-inch strips (see Note)

4 medium tomatoes, finely chopped (1 pound)

1 small onion, finely chopped

1 Anaheim, 2 jalapeño, or 4 serrano chilies, stemmed, seeded, and finely chopped

1 teaspoon dried epazote leaves or dried oregano

1 cup water

¼ teaspoon salt

¼ teaspoon black pepper

1 cup grated semisoft cheese, such as Monterey Jack, sharp white cheddar, or farmer's cheese, or crumbled queso fresco, or a mixture (3 ounces)

1 cup Homemade Thickened Cream (page 41) or crème fraîche

¼ cup chopped cilantro leaves (optional)

EMPANADAS

✸

MAKES 12 EMPANADAS

AFTER THE SPANISH BROUGHT WHEAT TO THE NEW WORLD, STAPLES OF THE TABLE EXPANDED BEYOND THE CORN KITCHEN. NOT ONLY WAS WHEAT FLOUR TURNED INTO TORTILLAS, EUROPEAN-STYLE BREADS AND PASTRIES APPEARED—WITH A MEXICAN FLAIR, OF COURSE! THE SMALL "HAND PIES" CALLED EMPANADAS, WHICH COME WITH BOTH SAVORY AND SWEET FILLINGS, ARE REMINISCENT OF OLD WORLD DELICACIES SUCH AS CORNISH PASTIES AND APPLE TURNOVERS. EMPANADAS ARE OFTEN DEEP-FRIED, BUT YOU CAN AVOID THE EXTRA OIL, AS I DO HERE, BY BAKING THEM.

Empanada Dough
2 cups unbleached all-purpose flour
1 teaspoon baking powder
½ teaspoon salt
½ cup vegetable oil
½ cup cold water

2 cups Savory Chickpea and Walnut
*   Empanada Filling (recipe follows)*
1 egg yolk whisked with 1 tablespoon
*   water*

Place the flour, baking powder, and salt in a large bowl and stir with a fork to mix well. Add the oil and mix with your hands or a fork until the mixture is crumbly. Add the water and mix some more until you have a moist dough, like pizza dough. Knead the dough in the bowl until it becomes a smooth ball, about 1 minute. Lift out the dough and wrap in plastic wrap. Set aside at room temperature for at least 20 minutes or up to several hours or refrigerate overnight and bring back to room temperature before continuing.

When ready to use, divide the dough into 12 equal parts and roll each part between your hands into a ball. On a lightly floured surface, roll out each ball into a circle 6 inches in diameter. Place a scant 2 tablespoons of filling in the center of each circle and fold the dough over to make a half-moon. Moisten the outer edge of the dough with water and press all around the edge with the tines of a fork to seal. Bake right away or cover with plastic wrap and refrigerate overnight.

When ready to bake, preheat the oven to 425 degrees F. Place the empanadas on an ungreased baking sheet and brush the tops with the egg yolk and water mixture. Bake until the tops are golden, the edges lightly browned, and the dough cooked all the way through, 20 to 25 minutes. Remove and serve right away or at room temperature.

NOTE: You can vary the diameter of the empanadas from 2 inches for cocktail tidbits to 5 inches for lunch or dinner portions. The baking time will vary accordingly.

SAVORY CHICKPEA AND WALNUT EMPANADA FILLING

✷

MAKES 2 CUPS

Heat the oil in a small skillet. Add the walnuts, onion, jalapeño, and cumin and cook over medium heat, stirring occasionally, until the onion wilts, 4 to 5 minutes. Transfer to a food processor, add the chickpeas, cream, and salt, and puree as smooth as possible. Use right away or cover and refrigerate overnight (not longer).

NOTE: The chickpea and walnut puree also makes a delightful tamale filler. For an extra treat, tuck 1 or 2 walnut halves in the puree before wrapping the tamale.

1 tablespoon peanut oil

½ cup shelled walnuts, coarsely chopped

½ small onion, finely chopped

1 jalapeño chili, stemmed and minced

½ teaspoon ground cumin

1½ cups cooked chickpeas (page 112)

½ cup heavy cream

¼ teaspoon salt

AN UNCLASSIC TOSTADA

✹

MAKES 6 TOSTADAS

THE CLASSIC TOSTADA, A MEAL ATOP A CRISP-FRIED TORTILLA, FEATURES BEANS AND SHREDDED MEAT WITH SALAD ACCOMPANIMENTS. I LIKE TO MAKE A FESTIVE VEGETARIAN DISPLAY, STARRING THE BEANS—MY FAVORITE BLACK ONES THAT ARE SO POPULAR IN OAXACA—AND REPLACING THE MEAT WITH GOLDEN RICE. THE SALAD PART IS ACCENTUATED WITH AN ARRAY OF MEXICAN CRUDITÉS. FRESH MANGO SLICES, GUACAMOLE, AND A PIQUANT SAUCE FOR EACH, TO PILE ON AS DESIRED, COMPLETE THE PICTURE. THE COLORS ALONE ARE ENOUGH TO FEED YOU. ONE TOSTADA, BY THE TIME YOU'VE HEAPED IT HIGH, SERVES FOR LUNCH.

Pour the oil into a large skillet and heat until sizzling. One at a time, fry the tortillas on both sides until crisp and lightly golden. Drain on paper towels.

To serve, place a spoonful of beans on one half of each crisped tortilla. Place a spoonful of rice next to the beans on the other half. Arrange 2 or 3 mango slices in the center. Sprinkle some cheese over the beans and some cilantro over the rice. Serve right away accompanied by the sauce, Guacamole, and crudités.

NOTE: To prepare the mango, cut it lengthwise through the pulp to the pit into quarters. Peel away the skin. Cut through the pulp to the pit in either direction to make slices as thick as you like, paring the slices off the pit as you go.

¼ cup vegetable oil

6 corn tortillas

3 cups cooked black beans (page 96)

3 cups Golden Rice (page 92)

1 ripe but still firm mango, peeled and sliced (see Note)

1 cup crumbled feta or cotija cheese

½ cup cilantro leaves

2 cups Piquant Sauce with Chipotle Chilies and Tamarind (page 30)

2 cups Guacamole (page 20)

Mexican Crudités (page 22)

TAMALES

✹

ON STREET CORNERS, AT PLAZA CARTS, IN CANTINAS, AT EVERY TURN, TASTY SURPRISE PACKAGES OF MASA DUMPLINGS WRAPPED IN LEAVES AND STEAMED TO PILLOWY SOFTNESS AWAIT THE MEXICO TRAVELER. THE LEAF MAY BE CORN, AVOCADO, SWISS CHARD, PLANTAIN, **HOJA SANTA**, AMONG OTHERS; THE DUMPLING MAY BE PLAIN OR FILLED. FOR HOME COOKING, TAMALES ARE CONSIDERED HOLIDAY FOOD. THEY ARE SERVED AT CHRISTMAS, NEW YEAR'S, AND OTHER SPECIAL EVENTS WHEN RELATIVES COME TOGETHER AND COOK TOGETHER. THE DAY BEGINS WITH SOAKING AND GRINDING THE CORN TO MAKE THE **NIXTAMAL** FOR THE **MASA** AND GOES ON FROM THERE WITH MUCH CONVIVIALITY UNTIL THERE ARE ENOUGH STEAMING TAMALES FOR ALL TO HAVE THEIR FILL. IN SMALL AMOUNTS, AND TAKING ADVANTAGE OF **MASA HARINA**, TAMALES ARE NOT DIFFICULT TO MAKE. EVEN WITHOUT THE BENEFIT OF EXTRA HANDS, YOU CAN TREAT YOUR GUESTS TO YOUR OWN HOME VERSION FOR ANY SPECIAL OCCASION YOU MAY HAVE.

2 cups water

12 tablespoons (1½ sticks) butter

2 cups masa harina

1½ teaspoons baking powder

¾ teaspoon salt

18 to 25 corn husks, fresh or dried,
soaked 30 minutes to soften if dried

2 cups Creamed Corn and Cheese
Tamale Filling or Black Bean and
Plantain Tamale Filling
(recipes follow) (optional)

8 tablespoons (1 stick) butter, melted
and kept warm

1 cup cilantro sprigs

Place the water and butter in a saucepan and heat until the butter melts.

Place the *masa harina*, baking powder, and salt in a large bowl and stir with a fork to mix well. Whisk in the water and butter, beating well as you go, until you have a mixture the consistency of a wet cake batter. Don't worry if it seems too wet at first; it will thicken as you work.

Pour about 2 inches of water into a steamer or other large pot (see Note) and bring to a boil.

Shake the corn husks to dry them a bit. Select 12 husks large enough to roll into a tube 1 to 1½ inches in diameter and lay them out on a counter. (Or select smaller husks and overlap two or three for each wrapper.) Place a full ¼ cup of the batter in the center of each husk and press it into a rectangle about 4½ x 2½ inches and ¼ inch thick. If filling the tamales, spread 2 tablespoons of the filling down the center of the batter. Roll up the husks lengthwise to enclose the filling. Fold the pointed ends under to the seam side.

Arrange the tamales, seam side down, in 1 or 2 layers on the steamer rack or a plate. Set the rack or plate in the pot and cover the tamales with a thick layer of husks. Reduce the heat to a simmer and cover the pot. Steam the tamales until cooked through, about 1 hour. The filling will no longer be moist and sticky and will pull away from the husks.

Serve the tamales warm in the husks, to be unwrapped as eaten, accompanied by the warm melted butter and cilantro sprigs on the side.

NOTE: You can easily jerry-rig a steamer for tamales. You need a large pot with a lid, 1 or 2 cans, both ends removed, and a plate or rack that will fit inside the pot. Fill the pot with about 2 inches of water. When ready to cook, set the cans in the pot to hold the plate above the water level. Arrange the tamales on the plate, set it on the cans, and cover the pot.

CREAMED CORN AND CHEESE TAMALE FILLING

✸

MAKES 2 CUPS

Place all the ingredients in a medium bowl and stir to mix. Use right away or store in the refrigerator overnight (not longer).

1 cup corn kernels (from 1 large or 2 small ears corn)

⅓ cup finely chopped onion

1 jalapeño chili, stemmed and finely chopped

1½ cups grated semisoft cheese, such as Monterey Jack, farmer's cheese, or queso asadero (4 to 5 ounces)

2 tablespoons heavy cream

BLACK BEAN AND PLANTAIN TAMALE FILLING

✸

MAKES 2 CUPS

In Oaxaca, black bean–filled tamales are wrapped in banana leaves and seasoned with *hoja santa* or anisy avocado leaves. To approximate the flavor, I combine plantain pulp with black beans and season the mixture with anise seed and bay leaf.

Heat the oil in a small skillet. Add the onion, garlic, anise seed and bay leaf, and sauté over medium heat until the onion is wilted, about 3 minutes. Transfer to a food processor, add the beans, plantain, and salt and puree as fine as possible. Use right away or cover and refrigerate overnight (not longer).

1 tablespoon peanut oil

½ small onion, finely chopped

2 garlic cloves, minced or pressed

⅛ teaspoon anise seed

1 bay leaf, minced

1½ cups cooked black beans with broth (page 96)

1 ripe medium plantain, peeled

½ teaspoon salt

chapter three

SOUPS

SUNNY SOUPS FROM SOUTH OF THE BORDER

❄

N O MATTER WHAT THE WEATHER, WARMING, BROTHY SOUP, AFLOAT WITH SOME BITS OF VEGETABLES, PERHAPS SOME RICE OR **MASA** DUMPLINGS OR PASTA, OPENS A MEXICAN RESTAURANT MEAL. At home, soup in heartier, more laden concoctions often constitutes the evening repast.

Traditionally, Mexican cooks rely on meat and poultry stocks, usually chicken but sometimes pork or beef, especially for the substantial, meal-type soups. But most important for making delicous soup in any style is to take seriously the maxim, "The soup is as good as the broth." In this collection of classic Mexican soup recipes, a healthful vegetable stock—earthy and sweet with carrots, onion, celery, and peas; bright with tomatoes, summer squash, and leafy greens; aromatic with herbs; mildly spiced with chili and garlic—replaces the customary meat or poultry broth. It's replete with flavor, fat free, and a splendid base for any of the sunny soups of Mexico.

VEGETABLE STOCK

✸

MAKES 12 CUPS (3 QUARTS)

THERE ARE TWO TRICKS TO ACHIEVING A DENSELY FLAVORFUL VEGETABLE STOCK: FIRST, DON'T STINT ON THE QUANTITY OF VEGETABLES. THE VEGETABLES YOU START WITH NEED NOT BE PICTURE-PERFECT, AS LONG AS THERE ARE ENOUGH TO JUST BARELY FLOAT FREELY IN THE AMOUNT OF WATER YOU ARE USING. SECOND, SIMMER THEM UNTIL THEY ARE VERY SOFT BUT NOT DISINTEGRATING. RAPID BOILING AND/OR OVERCOOKING RESULT IN A MURKY, STALE-TASTING BROTH. FOLLOWING THESE TWO GUIDELINES, YOU CAN TURN OUT A VEGETABLE BROTH RICH ENOUGH TO SERVE AS A BOUILLON ON ITS OWN OR PROVIDE THE BASE FOR ANY OF YOUR SOUP OR STOCK NEEDS.

Combine all the ingredients in a large pot and bring to a boil. Reduce the heat, partially cover, and simmer until the carrots are very soft and the broth is well colored, about 1 hour and 15 minutes.

Strain the stock through a sieve set over a large bowl, pressing down on the vegetables to extract all the juices. Discard the vegetables. Use the stock right away or cool, cover, and refrigerate for up to 1 week. Freeze for longer storage.

6 medium tomatoes, coarsely chopped
    (1½ pounds)

1 medium onion, unpeeled and quartered

2 large garlic cloves, halved

2 celery ribs, including tops, cut crosswise into 2-inch lengths

2 medium carrots, cut crosswise into 1-inch lengths

4 large or 8 medium chard leaves, cut crosswise into 2-inch shreds

12 whole pea pods

1 chayote or 2 medium zucchini, cut into 1-inch chunks

1 cup fresh parsley leaves

½ cup cilantro leaves

1 jalapeño chili, cut in half lengthwise

1 teaspoon fresh thyme leaves or
    ½ teaspoon dried thyme

1 bay leaf

1 teaspoon salt

14 cups water

TORTILLA SOUP

❋

SERVES 6

CLEVER COOKS OF THE EUROPEAN LATIN CULTURES—SPAIN, ITALY, FRANCE—INNOVATIVELY RECYCLE YESTERDAY'S STALE BREAD INTO TODAY'S DELICIOUS AND FILLING BREAD SOUPS. IN THE SEMI-LATIN CUISINE OF MEXICO, IT'S DAY-OLD TORTILLAS THAT ARE CREATIVELY, SATISFYINGLY REUSED FOR TORTILLA SOUP. TORTILLA SOUP IS ONE OF THOSE CLASSIC FAVORITES THAT ORIGINATED AS A HEARTH DISH AND WAS SO UNIVERSALLY APPEALING, IT BECAME EXPECTED FROM TIME TO TIME, NOT ONLY AT HOME, NOT ONLY TO BE ECONOMICAL, BUT ALSO IN PUBLIC EATING PLACES, INCLUDING FANCY RESTAURANTS. POPULAR THROUGHOUT MEXICO, TORTILLA SOUP IS SERVED EVERYWHERE.

1 pound tomatoes, peeled and seeded (page 14)

1 medium onion

1 large garlic clove

½ cup olive oil

2 large dried red chilies, preferably pasillas, stemmed, seeded, and cut into ⅛-inch strips

6 stale corn tortillas, cut into ½-inch strips

1 teaspoon chopped fresh marjoram leaves or ½ teaspoon dried marjoram

5 cups Vegetable Stock (page 69)

½ teaspoon salt

1 cup grated semisoft white cheese, such as sharp white cheddar, mozzarella, or queso panela (3 ounces)

Place the tomatoes, onion, and garlic in a food processor and puree as fine as possible. Set aside.

Heat the oil in a large pot until smoking. Add the chili strips and fry over high heat, stirring constantly, until toasted, 10 to 20 seconds only. Transfer to paper towels to drain. Set aside.

In the same pot, fry the tortilla strips in 2 or 3 batches over medium-high heat, stirring constantly, for 2 minutes, or until slightly golden and toasty. Transfer each batch to paper towels to drain. Set aside.

Add the tomato mixture and the marjoram to the pot and let bubble gently on medium heat for 5 minutes, or until slightly thickened and no longer raw. Stir in the stock and salt and simmer for 10 minutes, until well colored.

Add the tortilla strips and cheese. Bring to a boil and stir to mix and string out the cheese. Serve right away, sprinkled with the chili strips.

LENTIL AND CHARD SOUP

✸

SERVES 4 TO 6

QUICKLY SIMMERED TENDER IN A GOOD VEGETABLE STOCK, PLUMPED OUT WITH A HEAP OF SHREDDED CHARD LEAVES, AND FLOURISHED WITH CHEESE AND FRESH CHILIES, THE EARTH'S OLDEST CULTIVATED LEGUME, THE LENTIL, PROVIDES A NOURISHING, LOW-FAT, COMPLETE PROTEIN. DELICIOUS AS EVER, LENTILS MAKE A MEAL-IN-A-BOWL IN NO TIME FLAT.

6 cups Vegetable Stock (page 69)

1 cup lentils (6 ounces)

3 medium tomatoes, peeled (page 14)
  or 4 canned tomatoes, seeded and
  coarsely chopped, juices reserved
  (¾ pound)

¼ teaspoon salt

½ pound Swiss chard, coarsely chopped,
  rinsed, and drained (about 4 packed
  cups)

1 large jalapeño chili, stemmed and
  minced

½ cup crumbled feta cheese or queso
  añejo

Combine the stock, lentils, tomatoes, and salt in a large pot. Bring to a boil, partly cover, and simmer for 10 minutes, or until the lentils are partially cooked. Stir in the chard and simmer for 5 to 8 minutes, or until the lentils are cooked through and the chard is wilted.

Sprinkle the chili and cheese over the top and serve right away.

TOASTED GARLIC SOUP

✷

SERVES 4 TO 6

IN MANY A MARKETPLACE AND TOWN PLAZA IN MEXICO, AS YOU SHOP, PROMENADE, OR JUST WANDER AND GAWK, THE AROMA OF GARLIC SOUP BECKONS YOU. IT'S IRRESISTIBLE. YOU STOP—TO REST, REPLENISH, AND RESTORE YOURSELF WITH A BOWL OF IT—AND YOU REMEMBER TO MAKE SOME WHEN YOU GET HOME.

¼ cup olive oil

1 head garlic, cloves separated, peeled, and coarsely chopped

½ baguette, cut crosswise into ¼-inch-thick slices, or 6 slices other French bread

2 ancho chilies, stemmed, seeded, and coarsely chopped (1 ounce)

4 medium tomatoes, peeled and seeded (page 14) and coarsely chopped into ½-inch chunks (1 pound)

7 cups Vegetable Stock (page 69)

¾ teaspoon salt

½ cup Homemade Thickened Cream (page 41) or sour cream

Heat the oil in a large heavy skillet until smoking. Add the garlic and stir over medium-high heat for 1 minute, until lightly toasted. Transfer the garlic to a large soup pot.

Add as many slices of the bread to the skillet as will fit in one uncrowded layer. Fry over medium-high heat for 1 minute, turning once, until lightly golden on each side. Transfer to paper towels to drain. Continue until all the bread is fried. Set aside.

Place the chili peppers and tomatoes in the skillet and stir over medium-high heat for 1 minute, until wilted. Transfer to the soup pot with the garlic. Add the stock and salt, bring to a boil, and simmer for 20 minutes, or until the garlic is soft.

Ladle the soup into individual bowls. Garnish each bowl with fried bread and a dollop of cream. Serve right away, piping hot.

CORN CHOWDER

✳

SERVES 4 TO 6

SEASONED LIKE THE LIGHTER, BROTHIER **SOPA DE ELOTE** OF MEXICAN CUISINE, THIS CORN SOUP IS THICK WITH POTATOES AND MAKES A CHOWDERY BOWLFUL THAT FITS INTO THE MEAL AS AN APPETIZER OR FILLER, DEPENDING ON THE AMOUNT SERVED.

3 tablespoons butter

1 medium onion, finely chopped

2 cups corn kernels (from 2 large or 4 small ears corn)

2 cups milk

2 cups water

1 medium russet potato, peeled and coarsely cut into 1-inch chunks

¼ teaspoon salt

2 medium poblano chili peppers, roasted, stemmed, and peeled (page 13), then cut into ¼-inch dice (6 ounces)

¼ cup cilantro leaves

1 lime, cut into wedges

Heat the butter in a large pot until it melts. Stir in the onion and 1½ cups of the corn and sauté over medium heat for 5 minutes, or until the onion is soft. Add the milk, water, potato, and salt to the pot. Bring to a boil, reduce the heat, and simmer briskly until a skin forms on the soup and the potato mashes easily when pressed, about 15 minutes. Remove from the heat and cool completely. Puree the mixture.

Return the puree to the pot and stir in the chili pepper and remaining ½ cup of corn kernels. Bring to a boil again and simmer for 5 minutes, until the kernels are tender. Sprinkle the cilantro over the top and serve right away, accompanied by the lime wedges.

GREEN POZOLE

✹

SERVES 4 TO 6

WHEN PEELED KERNELS OF DRIED CORN ARE COOKED TENDER AND SERVED WHOLE, NOT GROUND, THEY ARE CALLED POZOLE. WHEN SIMMERED IN A SEASONED LIQUID AND SERVED WITH THE BROTH, THE CORN AND BROTH TOGETHER ARE ALSO CALLED POZOLE. AND THUS POZOLE HAS TWO MEANINGS. IT CAN REFER TO THE LARGE, FLINTY KERNELS OF CORN PROCESSED INTO **NIXTAMAL** OR TO THE HEARTY SOUP OF MEXICAN COOKING TRADITIONALLY SERVED AS A HANGOVER CURE AFTER TOO MUCH FESTIVITIES. IN A TASTY, EXTRASPICY VEGETABLE BROTH WITH PROTEIN-COMPLEMENTING GARNISHES, POZOLE SHINES AS A LIGHT MEAL, WHETHER YOU'VE PARTIED OR NOT.

Combine the tomatillos, chilies, onion, garlic, epazote, and stock in a large pot. Bring to a boil, partially cover, and simmer for 20 minutes, or until the onion is soft. Add the hominy and simmer for 5 minutes more, until heated through.

Arrange the pumpkin seeds, cheese, red onion, oregano, and tortillas on a platter.

Ladle the soup into individual bowls and serve piping hot. Pass the platter of garnishes at the table for each to add according to taste.

1 pound tomatillos, husked, rinsed, and coarsely chopped into ½-inch chunks

6 serrano chilies, stemmed and coarsely chopped

1 medium onion, coarsely chopped into ½-inch chunks

2 large garlic cloves, coarsely chopped

1 teaspoon chopped fresh epazote or sage leaves

6 cups Vegetable Stock (page 69)

3 cups cooked or canned and drained white hominy (29-ounce can)

¼ cup Toasted Pumpkin Seeds (page 21)

½ cup crumbled feta cheese or queso añejo

½ medium red or white onion, finely chopped

2 tablespoons chopped fresh oregano leaves or 2 teaspoons dried oregano

8 flour tortillas, warmed

SQUASH BLOSSOM SOUP

✵

SERVES 4 TO 6

IN MEXICO, SQUASH BLOSSOMS ARE FOR SALE BY THE POUND! ALMOST EVERY MARKET SPORTS A NEATLY MOUNDED PYRAMID, OR SEVERAL, OF VIBRANT YELLOW, FRAGRANT FLOWERS OF BOTH SUMMER AND WINTER SQUASH. **FLORS DE CALABAZA**, AS THEY ARE GENERICALLY CALLED, ARE A RARE TREAT NORTH OF THE BORDER. YET, SO PERVASIVE ARE THEY IN MEXICAN COOKING—FROM CHEESE-STUFFED FRITTERS TO QUESADILLAS TO SOUPS, BOTH BROTHY AND "DRY"—AND SO DELIGHTFUL A CULINARY TREAT, I INCLUDE THIS RECIPE AND ANOTHER FOR A **SOPA SECA** PASTA DISH FEATURING THEM, SPAGHETTI A LA PRIMAVERA MEXICANA (PAGE 90), IN CASE YOU HAVE A MARKET THAT OFFERS THEM OR A GARDEN PLANT OR TWO FROM WHICH TO PICK YOUR OWN (SEE NOTE).

2 tablespoons butter

1 medium white onion, chopped into
    ¼-inch dice

2 large garlic cloves, finely chopped

1 teaspoon dried marjoram leaves

2 medium tomatoes, peeled and seeded
    (page 14), finely chopped

¾ pound squash blossoms, coarsely
    chopped

4 to 6 tiny zucchini or other summer
    squash, halved lengthwise (½ pound)

1 small jalapeño chili, stemmed and very
    thinly shredded

½ teaspoon salt

8 cups Vegetable Stock (page 69)

¼ cup chopped cilantro leaves

Melt the butter in a large heavy pot over medium heat. Add the onion, garlic, and marjoram and sauté gently until barely wilted, about 1 minute. Stir in the tomatoes and cook gently until they begin to soften, about 1 minute. Stir in the squash blossoms and sauté until wilted, about 2 minutes.

Add the zucchini, jalapeño, salt, and stock and bring to a boil. Simmer until the vegetables are barely soft, about 10 minutes. Stir in the cilantro and serve right away.

NOTES: Ideally, only the male squash flowers, which do not develop fruit, are selected for cooking—the male blossom has a narrow stem; the female has a bulge at the base which eventually becomes the squash—but you can pick the female blossoms, too, if you are willing to sacrifice the squash itself. To prepare squash blossoms, simply rinse them, shake them dry, and chop or shred them, along with their stems.

Though butter is not an ordinary ingredient in a Mexican soup, I use it here because it enhances the delicacy of the squash blossoms, which would be overwhelmed by olive oil.

MELON AND POTATO SOUP

✹

SERVES 6

UNLIKELY AS THE COMBINATION MAY SEEM, MELON AND POTATOES MELD TOGETHER IN A DELEC-
TABLE, SMOOTH SOUP THAT STANDS OUT AS AN EXAMPLE OF HOW THE OLD AND THE NEW MERGE
IN A SURPRISING AND PLEASING WAY, AS THEY SO OFTEN DO IN MEXICO.

¼ cup slivered almonds

1½ pounds russet potatoes, peeled and
    coarsely chopped into ½-inch chunks

4 cups milk

1 serrano chili, stemmed and halved

½ teaspoon salt

1 medium cantaloupe, halved, seeds
    removed, pulp scooped out (see Note)

1 lime, cut into 6 thin rounds

Spread the almonds in a heated ungreased skillet or on a microwave-safe plate.
Stir over medium-high heat or microwave, uncovered, on high until toasted,
about 3 minutes. Let cool. Coarsely chop and set aside.

Put the potatoes, milk, chili pepper, and salt in a large pot. Bring to a boil,
reduce the heat, partly cover, and simmer until the potatoes are almost disintegrating, about 15 minutes. Set aside to cool to room temperature. Remove and
discard the chili pepper pieces. Puree the potato mixture with the melon pulp.
Return the puree to the pot or a microwave-safe bowl and reheat.

Ladle the soup into individual bowls. Sprinkle the chopped almonds over the
top and float a lime slice to the side in each bowl. Serve right away.

NOTE: When scooping out the melon pulp, take care to avoid the green part
next to the rind. It will lend an unpleasing bitter note to the soup.

AVOCADO VICHYSSOISE

❋

SERVES 6

A THIN PUREE OF LEEKS AND POTATOES, CHILLED, SERVED IN A BOWL, AND CALLED **VICHYSSOISE** IN FRENCH, ENJOYS A REPUTATION AS ONE OF **THE** ELEGANT SOUPS. ITS TONGUE-TWISTING (TO NON-FRENCH SPEAKERS) NAME BELIES ITS HUMBLE FOUNDATIONS. SIMPLE AND STRAIGHTFORWARD, AT THE SAME TIME REFRESHING AND SUAVE, ITS REPUTATION IS WELL COME BY. IN THIS SOUTH-OF-THE-BORDER VERSION, VICHYSSOISE STAYS COOL AND BECOMES EVEN MORE UNCTUOUS WITH AVOCADO. IT'S RICH ENOUGH TO SATISFY A MIDDAY HUNGER AND BREEZY ENOUGH TO BEGIN A SUMMER NIGHT REPAST.

Place the potatoes, leek, thyme, salt, and water in a large pot. Bring to a boil, reduce the heat, and simmer for 15 minutes, or until the potatoes are soft all the way through. Set aside to cool to room temperature, then refrigerate to chill thoroughly, up to overnight.

Using a food processor, puree the potato mixture with the avocado, in batches. Transfer the puree to a large bowl. Return the puree to the refrigerator to rechill for 1 hour or so before serving.

Just before serving, stir in the lime juice. Ladle the soup into individual bowls and garnish with a dollop of cream and a sprinkling of chives.

2 medium russet potatoes, peeled and
    coarsely chopped into ½-inch chunks
    (¾ pound)
1 large or 2 small leeks, trimmed,
    washed, and cut into ½-inch pieces
1 teaspoon chopped fresh thyme leaves or
    ½ teaspoon dried thyme
1 teaspoon salt
6 cups water
3 medium avocados, peeled and pitted
¼ cup fresh lime juice
½ cup Homemade Thickened Cream
    (page 41) or sour cream
¼ cup chopped chives

MEXICAN GAZPACHO

✹

SERVES 6

JUICED TOMATOES, CHILI, LIME, AND TEQUILA. IT SOUNDS LIKE THE MAKINGS OF A GOOD LIQUID REFRESHMENT. IT IS. WITH EXTRA VEGETABLES—CUCUMBER, PEPPER, ONION, GARLIC—SOME HERB STIRRED IN (OREGANO IS GOOD) AND A CRUNCHY GARNISH OF AVOCADO-TOPPED FLOUR TORTILLA CHIPS, THE CLASSIC ICED SOUP OF SPAIN COMES TOGETHER AS MEXICAN GAZPACHO.

In a large bowl stir together the tomatoes, stock, lime juice, cucumber, chilies, scallions, garlic, and 1 teaspoon of the fresh oregano or ½ teaspoon dried. Cover and refrigerate for several hours or overnight, until very cold.

Just before serving, stir in the olive oil, salt to taste, and tequila, if using. Spread the chopped avocado on the tortilla chips and sprinkle the remaining fresh oregano or other herb over the avocado. Ladle the soup into individual bowls. Garnish each bowl with the avocado-topped chips and serve right away.

NOTE: An equally fine, and also traditional, gazpacho can be made without pureeing and straining the tomatoes. Increase the amount of Vegetable Stock to 4 cups. Peel and seed 2 pounds of tomatoes and cut them into thin julienne strips. Stir the tomatoes into the stock along with the other vegetables.

3 pounds ripe tomatoes, peeled and
   seeded (page 14), pureed, and
   strained (see Note)
2 cups Vegetable Stock (page 69)
   or water
½ cup fresh lime juice
1 medium cucumber, peeled, seeded, and
   finely chopped
1 medium Anaheim chili, stemmed,
   seeded, and finely chopped
1 jalapeño chili, stemmed, seeded, and
   finely chopped
4 scallions, trimmed and minced
1 large garlic clove, minced or pressed
1 tablespoon chopped fresh oregano leaves
   or ½ teaspoon dried oregano plus 1
   tablespoon chopped fresh parsley or
   cilantro leaves
2 tablespoons olive oil
Salt, to taste
1 tablespoon tequila (optional)
1 medium avocado, peeled, pitted, and
   coarsely chopped
½ recipe Tortilla Chips (page 49),
   made with flour tortillas

chapter four

PASTA, RICE
& BEANS

STAPLES OF THE MEXICAN VEGETARIAN TABLE

※

PASTA, RICE, BEANS—ONE ALONE OR TWO IN COMBINATION—ARE ALWAYS PART OF A MEXICAN MEAL. Mexican cooks make glorious use of them and prepare them in myriad ways. Along with corn, they are the staples of Mexican cuisine. Pastas and rice, usually classified together as *sopas secas,* or "dry soups," in Mexican cooking, may be served as a separate course after a brothy soup and before the meat in a nonvegetarian meal. More elaborately prepared, such a dish may be the meal. The ever-present beans are similarly widely used: Atop a rice concoction, they may constitute the entire repast; mashed and fried, they may accompany the main course. Or they may be offered separately at the end—presumably to satisfy any lingering hunger!

In this chapter I include recipes for the beloved traditional rice and beans staples of Mexico and also a few of my own *sopa seca* concoctions in keeping with the style of Mexican cooking. I step outside tradition altogether and add a Mexican pilaf and a favorite cornmeal preparation I call Mexican Polenta. All can serve as a side dish or an entire meal.

SPAGHETTI WITH SPINACH, CHILIES, CREAM, AND ALMONDS

❈

SERVES 4 TO 6

DRY SOUPS PROVIDE A PERFECT MEDIUM IN WHICH TO BLEND INNOVATION AND TRADITION. USING WHATEVER YOU HAVE AT HAND, THEY LEND THEMSELVES TO WHIMSICAL COMBINATIONS FROM YOUR REFRIGERATOR AND PANTRY SHELVES. HERE, ROASTED CHILIES TOSSED WITH SPAGHETTI AND SPINACH KEEPS THE DISH SPUNKY, IN THE MEXICAN STYLE. THE CREAM MAKES IT SWEET AND RICH ENOUGH FOR A COMPANY MEAL.

Spread the almonds in an ungreased medium skillet or on a microwave-safe plate. Stir over medium-high heat or microwave on high for 5 minutes, until toasted. Set aside.

Coarsely chop the spinach leaves. Swish them about in plenty of cold water, then allow the water to come to rest. Lift the leaves out of the water and transfer to a colander. Set aside to drain without spinning—the leaves should remain moist.

Using a food processor, finely grind ⅔ cup of the almonds. Add the chilies, cream, and salt and puree as fine as possible. Set aside.

Heat the oil in a large heavy nonreactive pot. Add the garlic and oregano and stir constantly over medium-high heat until the garlic begins to brown, about 30 seconds. Add the spinach and stir over medium-high heat until the spinach wilts, 1 to 2 minutes.

Add the cream mixture and stir until boiling. Reduce the heat and simmer for 1 or 2 minutes until the mixture is bubbly and thickened. Stir in the spaghetti.

Sprinkle the remaining ⅓ cup almonds over the top and serve right away.

1 cup slivered almonds (4 ounces)

1½ pounds spinach, leaves only (about 2 bunches)

2 poblano chilies, roasted, peeled, and seeded (page 13)

1½ cups Homemade Thickened Cream (page 41) or 1 cup heavy cream

½ teaspoon salt

2 tablespoons peanut or olive oil

3 large garlic cloves, minced or pressed

1½ teaspoons chopped fresh oregano leaves or ¾ teaspoon dried oregano

1 pound spaghetti, cooked and drained

VERMICELLI WITH TOMATOES AND CHIPOTLE CHILIES

✺

SERVES 4 TO 6

THE PASTA NOODLE DISHES IN MEXICO ARE NOT QUITE SO SAUCY AS IN ITALY. THEY HAVE AN EXTRA HINT OF SPICE AND THEY'RE COOKED A LITTLE SOFTER, NOT **AL DENTE**. OTHERWISE, THEY RESEMBLE AND ARE SERVED THE SAME WAY AS THEIR ITALIAN COUNTERPARTS. VERY THIN VERMICELLI OR ANGEL HAIR PASTA, WITH THE MUSICAL NAME **FIDEO** IN SPANISH, IS PARTICULARLY APPRECIATED FOR RELAXED, INFORMAL EVENINGS.

Pour the oil into a large pot and heat until it begins to smoke. Add the vermicelli and stir-fry over high heat until well coated and starting to turn golden, about 1 minute. Add the onion and garlic and continue stirring until the onion wilts slightly, 1 minute. Add the tomatoes, chili, oregano, salt, and pepper and simmer until the tomatoes wilt, about 3 minutes.

Stir in the stock and bring to a boil. Reduce the heat and simmer until most of the liquid is absorbed, about 15 minutes. Transfer to a serving dish. Sprinkle the cheese and parsley over the top and serve right away.

¼ cup peanut or olive oil

½ pound vermicelli, broken up

1 small onion, finely chopped

2 garlic cloves, minced or pressed

3 medium tomatoes, peeled (page 14) and coarsely chopped into ¼-inch chunks (¾ pound)

1 canned chipotle chili, finely chopped

1 teaspoon chopped fresh oregano leaves or ½ teaspoon dried oregano

½ teaspoon salt

¼ teaspoon black pepper

4 cups Vegetable Stock (page 69)

1 cup grated Parmesan cheese (4 ounces)

½ cup chopped fresh parsley leaves

MACARONI AND CHEESE MEXICAN-STYLE

✸

SERVES 4 TO 6

SILKEN WITH THICK CREAM, STRINGY WITH MELTED CHEESE, AND TANGY WITH TOMATO AND CHILI PEPPER, MACARONI AND CHEESE MEXICAN-STYLE TAKES ON A SOFT, ROSY HUE. SOMETIMES CALLED **MACARRONES CASERO**, THE NAME IS APT—IT'S AN UNCOMPLICATED HOME DISH YOU CAN DO QUICKLY WHEN PEOPLE NEED TO EAT, AND SOON.

½ cup Vegetable Stock (page 69)

3 medium tomatoes, coarsely chopped
    into ¼-inch chunks (¾ pound)

½ medium onion, finely chopped

½ cup chopped fresh parsley leaves

1 teaspoon chopped fresh oregano leaves
    or ½ teaspoon dried oregano

1 bay leaf, finely crumbled

2 teaspoons paprika

1 teaspoon salt

¾ cup Homemade Thickened Cream
    (page 41) or sour cream

½ cup grated queso asadero or
    mozzarella cheese

¾ pound macaroni, cooked and drained

Heat the stock in a large pot. Add the tomatoes, onion, parsley, oregano, bay leaf, paprika, and salt and simmer until the vegetables soften, about 2 minutes. Stir in the cream and cheese and simmer until the cheese melts, about 1 minute. Stir in the macaroni and serve right away.

NOTE: To make a quick dish even quicker, chop the vegetables and fresh herbs together in a food processor. Put the onion, cut into 1-inch chunks, in first. Add the parsley and oregano, then the tomatoes, cut up a bit also, on top. Process in pulses until the onions are finely chopped and the tomatoes are coarse. Combine with the stock in a large pot and continue with the recipe.

SPAGHETTI A LA PRIMAVERA MEXICANA

✳

SERVES 4 TO 6

IN MEXICO, AS EVERYWHERE, SPRING PEEKS OUT TENDERLY, AND THE FIRST EDIBLE PRODUCTS OF THE NEW SEASON OFFER GENTLE RATHER THAN ROBUST COLORS AND FLAVORS. IN A PRIMAVERA MIX, BABY LIMA BEANS, SWEET YOUNG GARLIC, TINY SQUASH, AND A SUNNY SPLASH OF SQUASH FLOWERS COMBINE TO MAKE A LIGHT GREEN, SOFT YELLOW, DELICATE PASTA DISH.

2 tablespoons peanut or olive oil

8 small garlic cloves, slivered

1½ cups cooked baby lima beans
    (see Note)

¾ pound summer squash, preferably
    baby squash, trimmed and cut into
    ¼-inch rounds or wedges

¼ pound squash flowers, rinsed and
    coarsely chopped

1 small green or yellow chili, such as
    jalapeño or güero, stemmed, seeded,
    and finely chopped

½ teaspoon salt

2 cups Vegetable Stock (page 69)

1 pound spaghetti, cooked and drained

½ cup grated queso asadero or
    Parmesan cheese

Heat the oil in a large heavy nonreactive skillet. Add the garlic and stir over medium-high heat until turning golden, about 30 seconds. Transfer to paper towels to drain. Set aside.

Stir in the lima beans, squash, flowers, chili, and salt. Add the stock and bring to a boil. Reduce the heat and simmer until the vegetables are tender but still brightly colored.

Stir in the spaghetti and cook until heated through. Sprinkle the cheese and toasted garlic over the top and serve right away.

NOTE: For the lima beans, small and fresh are best, of course. You can often find them vacuum-wrapped in plastic bags in produce markets in the spring and early summer. Or you can start with ½ cup dried baby limas and place them in a pot with 4 cups water. Bring to a boil, then simmer until tender, 40 to 50 minutes. Or you can substitute frozen baby limas, which are acceptable though not as earthy tasting. The equivalent for the recipe is ½ cup. Use them directly from the package, without precooking.

WHITE RICE

✺

SERVES 6

WHITE RICE IN MEXICO, **ARROZ BLANCO**, IS NOT WHAT WE NORMALLY THINK OF AS STEAMED RICE. SPECKLED WITH TINY BITS OF CARROT, PEAS, CORN, OR ALL THREE, IT'S MORE LIKE MOTTLED RICE. **ARROZ BLANCO** IS COLORFUL.

Place the rice in a large bowl, add warm water to cover amply, and set aside to soak for 15 minutes. Drain, shake well, and set aside to drain for 5 minutes.

Heat the oil in a heavy, medium-sized pot. Add the rice and stir over medium-high heat until the grains become translucent, about 2 minutes. Add the onion and garlic and stir until the rice is golden around the edges, about 3 minutes. Add the stock, salt, and vegetables and bring to a boil. Reduce the heat to maintain the barest simmer, cover the pot, and cook without disturbing until the liquid is absorbed and the rice is tender, 17 to 20 minutes.

Remove from the heat and set aside to steam dry for an additional 15 minutes. Serve right away.

NOTE: For all Mexican rice dishes, the grains are soaked, drained, and sautéed before steaming, then cooked with onion and garlic, as one would make a pilaf. This method produces fluffy, separate grains and a nutty, full flavor befitting the major role rice plays in main meal offerings.

2 cups long-grain white rice

3 tablespoons peanut or olive oil

½ small onion, finely chopped

1 small garlic clove, minced or pressed

4 cups Vegetable Stock (page 69) or water

¼ teaspoon salt

1 cup peas, corn, or finely diced carrot, or a mixture

GOLDEN RICE

❋

SERVES 6

THE GOLD IN GOLDEN RICE IS NOT A METALLIC GOLD BUT AN EARTH-TONE OCHRE. IT'S PROVIDED BY ANNATTO, EITHER IN SEED FORM OR GROUND AND MIXED INTO THE SPICE PASTE CALLED ACHIOTE (PAGE 12). EITHER WAY, ANNATTO LENDS A SUBDUED TASTE AND COLOR SIMILAR TO SAFFRON, BUT AT LESS EXPENSE.

2 cups long-grain white rice

3 tablespoons peanut or olive oil

2 tablespoons annatto seeds or ½ tablespoon achiote paste

½ small onion, finely chopped

¼ teaspoon salt

4 cups water

Soak and drain the rice as described on page 91.

Heat the oil in a heavy, medium-sized pot. If using annatto seeds, put them in the pot and stir over low heat until the seeds are toasted and the oil is orange-yellow-red. Remove the seeds with a slotted spoon and discard them.

Stir the rice into the oil, add the achiote paste, if using, and stir over medium-high heat until the grains become translucent, about 2 minutes. Add the onion and continue stirring until the rice is golden around the edges, about 3 minutes. Add the salt and water and bring to a boil. Reduce the heat to maintain the barest simmer, cover the pot, and cook without disturbing until the liquid is absorbed and the rice is tender, 17 to 20 minutes.

Remove from the heat and set aside to steam dry for an additional 15 minutes. Serve right away.

MEXICAN RICE

❋

SERVES 6

YOU MAY REMEMBER MEXICAN RICE FROM THE CAFETERIA FOOD OF SCHOOL DAYS. NOSTALGIA ASIDE, THAT VERSION WOULD PROBABLY BE A DISAPPOINTMENT. BUT WHEN PROPERLY PREPARED, IMBUED WITH HOMEMADE VEGETABLE STOCK AND FLUFFED TO PERFECTION, IT'S A SUITABLE AND JUSTIFIABLE DISH, BOTH FOR DINNER AND FOR MEMORY.

Soak and drain the rice as described on page 91.

Using a food processor, puree the tomato, onion, garlic, and jalapeño. Set aside.

Heat the oil in a heavy, medium-sized pot. Add the rice and stir over medium-high heat until the grains become translucent. Add the tomato puree and stir until the mixture is no longer wet, about 5 minutes. Stir in the stock and salt and bring to a boil. Reduce the heat to maintain the barest simmer, cover the pot, and cook without disturbing until the liquid is absorbed and the rice is tender, 17 to 20 minutes. Stir in the peas and fluff the rice with a fork.

Cover the pot and set aside to steam dry for 15 minutes. Serve right away, garnished with the cilantro.

2 cups long-grain white rice

2 medium tomatoes (½ pound)

½ small onion

1 garlic clove

1 jalapeño or 2 serrano chilies, stemmed

3 tablespoons peanut or olive oil

4 cups Vegetable Stock (page 69)

¼ teaspoon salt

½ cup shelled fresh peas, blanched 3 minutes in boiling water and drained

½ cup cilantro leaves

MEXICAN PILAF

✺

SERVES 6

A TOASTY, LIGHT AND AIRY MOUND OF RICE INTERWOVEN WITH GOLDEN-BROWN VERMICELLI STRANDS, STEAMED TO PERFECTION, AND PEPPERED ONLY AT THE LAST MINUTE FOR MAXIMUM AROMA OFTEN ROUNDED OUT A MEAL, FAMILY OR FESTIVE, IN MY HALF-ARMENIAN CHILDHOOD. PILAF WAS A STANDARD DISH AND NO ONE COULD MAKE IT BETTER THAN MY NON-ARMENIAN MOTHER. LATER, I DISCOVERED PILAF CONCOCTIONS AROUND THE WORLD THAT INCLUDED ONION, NUTS, AND GRAINS OTHER THAN RICE. TO THIS DAY, I LOVE A PILAF, AND WHEN I THINK OF IT IN A MEXICAN MODE, I KEEP THE RICE FOR GRAIN, ADD PECANS, AND SPRINKLE CILANTRO OVER THE TOP (TRAVEL IS BROADENING, MOM).

1½ cups long-grain white rice

⅓ cup peanut oil

2 tablespoons butter

1 cup broken-up vermicelli (2 ounces)

½ cup finely chopped onion

1 cup pecans, coarsely chopped
  (4 ounces)

3 cups water

½ teaspoon salt

¼ cup chopped cilantro leaves

Soak and drain the rice as described on page 91.

Heat the oil and butter in a heavy, medium-sized pot. Add the vermicelli, onion, and pecans and stir over medium-high heat until the vermicelli turns golden, about 2 minutes. Stir in the rice, mixing well. Add the water and salt and bring to a boil. Reduce the heat, cover the pot, and simmer without disturbing until the liquid is absorbed and the rice is tender, about 20 minutes.

Remove from the heat and set aside to steam dry for 15 minutes. Sprinkle the cilantro over the top and serve right away.

MEXICAN POLENTA

✹

I N MEXICAN POLENTA, THE OLD AND NEW WORLD WAYS WITH GROUND CORN MERGE INTO A CULINARY TWOSOME MADE IN HEAVEN. CORNMEAL OR POLENTA — EITHER WILL DO — IS COOKED INTO A CREAMY, SOFT, MUSH LACED WITH SOUTH-OF-THE-BORDER FLAVORS AND FINISHED TO PERFECTION WITH RED ENCHILADA SAUCE.

Melt the butter in a large microwave-safe dish or heavy pot. Stir in the corn kernels, onion, jalapeño, and sage and microwave or sauté until the corn softens, about 4 minutes. Stir in the cornmeal, water, and salt and cook, uncovered, until the mixture barely begins to thicken, about 20 minutes on the stove top, stirring frequently, or 4 minutes in the microwave. Stir to mix and smooth out the lumps. Cook until the mixture is thick but still pourable, 10 to 15 minutes on the stove top, 5 minutes in the microwave (see Note).

Spoon the sauce over the top, sprinkle on the cheese, and serve right away.

NOTE: With a microwave, the time spent making Mexican Polenta is significantly shorter than for stove top cooking, and the fret of hovering over the pan and stirring almost constantly to prevent sticking is eliminated. Microwave directions are for the high setting.

3 tablespoons butter

2 cups corn kernels (from 3 large ears corn)

¼ cup finely chopped onion

1 large jalapeño chili, stemmed and finely chopped

½ teaspoon dried sage

1 cup yellow cornmeal or polenta

3 cups water

¾ teaspoon salt

2 cups Red Enchilada Sauce (page 57)

½ cup grated Monterey Jack cheese (2 ounces)

POT BEANS

✹

MAKES 6 CUPS

PINK, PINTO, SPECKLED, BLACK, LONG AND KIDNEY-SHAPED, OR SHORT AND ROUND, IN MEXICO, DRIED BEANS OF ONE SORT OR ANOTHER ARE PROBABLY COOKED IN EVERY KITCHEN EVERY DAY. THE BASIC METHOD CALLS FOR SIMMERING THE BEANS IN PLENTY OF WATER WITH ONION AND GARLIC, MAYBE SOME EPAZOTE, AND SALT, WHICH IS ADDED ONLY AT THE END SO THAT THE BEANS WON'T TOUGHEN. THE BEANS ARE NOT PRESOAKED. THE LIQUID IS NEVER DRAINED AWAY, AND THE BEANS, IF MADE IN ADVANCE, ARE STORED IN THEIR COOKING LIQUID. THIS LIQUID IS EITHER INCORPORATED INTO THE DISH OR USED AS BROTH FOR ANOTHER DISH.

2 cups dried beans (¾ pound)

1 large onion, quartered

2 large garlic cloves, unpeeled and halved

10 cups water

2 teaspoons fresh epazote leaves or 1 teaspoon dried epazote (optional)

1 teaspoon salt

Combine the beans, onion, garlic, water, and epazote, if using, in a large pot and bring to a boil. Reduce the heat, partly cover, and simmer until the beans are slightly soft but not tender all the way through, 45 minutes to 1 hour and 15 minutes, depending on the age and type of beans.

Add the salt and cook, uncovered, for 15 minutes, or until the beans are tender all the way through, easily mashed, and still immersed in the liquid but not floating freely. Serve right away or cool, cover, and refrigerate for up to several days. Remove the onion, garlic, and epazote, if any, before serving.

WELL-FRIED BEANS WITH CHEESE
AND FRESH RED CHILIES

✸

SERVES 4 TO 6

THE NAME OF THE DISH **FRIJOLES REFRITOS** IS COMMONLY MISTRANSLATED AS "REFRIED BEANS." ACTUALLY, THE BEANS ARE FRIED ONLY ONCE, THE "RE" HERE MEANING DONE THOROUGHLY OR COMPLETELY RATHER THAN AGAIN. SEMANTICS ASIDE, WHEN YOU START WITH YOUR OWN HOMEMADE POT BEANS, MASH AND THICKEN THEM, AND ADD A GOOD SHARP CHEESE TO GILD THE TOP, YOU HAVE A SAVORY BEAN PUDDING THAT CAN BE SERVED ON THE SIDE OR AS A STICK-TO-THE-RIBS MEAL.

Heat the oil in a large heavy skillet. Add the onion and garlic and stir over medium heat until slightly golden, about 5 minutes. Add the beans and some of the broth, a cup at a time, mashing the beans with a fork, slotted spoon, or potato masher as you go. Stir the mixture over medium heat until thickened to a paste but not dried out, 15 to 20 minutes. Stir in the salt and sprinkle the cheese and chilies over the top. Serve right away.

3 tablespoons peanut or olive oil

½ small onion, finely chopped

1 garlic clove, minced or pressed

3 cups Pot Beans, including the liquid (page 96)

½ teaspoon salt

½ cup crumbled queso fresco, feta, or kasseri cheese or 1 cup grated sharp cheddar or Monterey Jack cheese

1 to 2 small fresh chilies, red if possible, for color, stemmed and minced

BEAN CAKES

✸

SERVES 6

FOR EXCELLENT SNACKING MORSELS, TAKE YOUR LEFTOVER POT BEANS, STRAIN THEM A LITTLE DRIER THAN YOU WOULD FOR **FRIJOLES REFRITOS**, MASH THEM, AND FORM THEM INTO PATTIES. BROWN THE PATTIES UNTIL YOU HAVE A CRUNCHY CRUST. FOR A PARTY, MAKE A POT OF BEANS SPECIFICALLY FOR BEAN CAKES. ARRANGE THE PATTIES ON A PLATTER, PUT A DOLLOP OF SALSA AND ONE OF CREAM ON TOP OF EACH, AND SPRINKLE CHOPPED PARSLEY OR CILANTRO LEAVES OVER ALL FOR COLOR.

Using a food processor or potato masher, mash the beans to a textured puree. Transfer to a bowl and stir in the onion, chilies, cumin, and salt. Form ¼-cup amounts of the bean mixture into 3-by-½-inch patties, or make smaller patties for easy-to-handle party fare.

Heat 2 tablespoons of the oil in a large heavy skillet. Put as many patties in the skillet as will fit in a single uncrowded layer and fry over fairly high heat until golden and toasty, about 1 minute per side. Transfer to a platter. Continue until all the patties are fried, adding more oil to the skillet as necessary.

Serve right away, accompanied by the salsa and cream on the side.

1 recipe Pot Beans (page 96), well drained

1 medium white onion, minced

2 serrano chilies, stemmed and minced

¼ teaspoon ground cumin

½ teaspoon salt

¼ cup peanut oil

1 cup Fresh Tomato Salsa (page 24)

1 cup Homemade Thickened Cream (page 41)

FAVA BEAN STEW

✺

SERVES 6

THE FAVA BEAN IS AN OLD WORLD BEAN, THE ONLY ONE, IN FACT. LONG-USED BOTH AS A FALLOW CROP TO FIX NITROGEN IN A FIELD THAT NEEDS REPLENISHING AND AS A SOURCE OF HUMAN NOURISHMENT, FAVAS HAVE BEEN INCORPORATED INTO MEXICAN COOKING, ESPECIALLY FOR LENT WHEN ONE IS SUPPOSED TO ABSTAIN FROM THE PLEASURES OF FLESH. SIMILAR TO THE NEW WORLD LIMAS, FAVAS—ALSO CALLED BROAD BEANS—ARE LARGE, "MEATY," FLAVORFUL BEANS, EXCELLENT FOR STEWING INTO A HEARTY **SOPA SECA**. A HELPING OF THE DISH SUFFICES FOR A COMPLETELY SATIS-FYING, MEATLESS MEAL.

4 pounds fresh fava beans in the pods, shelled

¼ cup olive oil

1 large onion, coarsely chopped into ¼-inch chunks

6 garlic cloves, coarsely chopped

1 large jalapeño chili, stemmed and coarsely chopped

½ teaspoon ground cumin

1½ pounds tomatoes, peeled (page 14) and coarsely chopped

½ teaspoon salt

2 cups water

½ cup chopped mint leaves

½ cup crumbled queso añejo, feta, or kasseri cheese (2 ounces)

Bring a large pot of water to a boil. Drop the beans into the water and bring back to a boil. Cook for 3 minutes. Drain and let cool. If the favas are large and the outer skins tough, peel them with your fingers. If the beans are small and tender, use as is.

Heat the oil in a large heavy pot. Add the onion, garlic, chili, and cumin and sauté until the onion wilts, about 5 minutes. Stir in the tomatoes, salt, water, and ¼ cup of the mint. Bring to a boil, reduce the heat, and simmer until the tomatoes soften, about 5 minutes. Add the fava beans and simmer for 10 minutes, or until the beans are very tender.

Ladle the stew into individual bowls. Sprinkle the cheese and remaining mint over the top and serve right away.

NOTE: Dried fava beans may be substituted for the fresh. Cook ¾ pound dried favas as for Pot Beans (page 96). Drain, cool, and peel them, and proceed with the recipe.

chapter five

SALADS &
VEGETABLES

THE HEART OF THE MATTER

❋

IN THE HEART OF A MEXICAN MARKET, AWE TURNS INTO ENERGY AS THE SIGHTS, SOUNDS, AND SMELLS, AND THE BOUNTIFUL, GRANDLY STYLED AND HIGHLY ARRANGED DISPLAYS SET ME ITCHING TO COOK. The recipes in this chapter pay tribute to the glorious offerings of the Mexican land and the traditions of Mexican cooking. At the same time, the recipes often bend custom to emphasize lighter, more streamlined fare to suit modern health and time considerations. I hope that if you love food and cooking, you, too, will be inspired to fill your basket with vegetables and get right to work in the kitchen, with a Mexican flair!

SPINACH SALAD WITH PINE NUTS, CHEESE, AND MINT VINAIGRETTE

❋

SERVES 6

BESIDES ROMAINE, SPINACH IS THE OTHER COMMON LEAF SALAD IN MEXICO. IT'S ESPECIALLY POPULAR MOISTENED WITH A MINT AND CHEESE DRESSING, AND RIGHTLY SO. THE COMBINATION IS A NATURAL. I'VE ADDED THE PINE NUTS TO SOFTEN THE ASSERTIVE FLAVOR COMBINATION OF SPINACH, MINT, AND TANGY CHEESE.

Place the pine nuts in a heated ungreased medium skillet or spread them on a microwave-safe plate. Stir over medium-high heat or microwave, uncovered, on high until slightly golden and toasted, about 5 minutes. Set aside.

Spread the spinach leaves on a platter or individual plates. Arrange the tomatoes to one side and the onions to the other. Sprinkle the pine nuts and cheese over all, drizzle on the vinaigrette, and serve right away.

½ cup pine nuts

1½ pounds spinach, tender leaves only, washed and dried

3 medium tomatoes, sliced (¾ pound)

1 recipe Wilted Red Onions (page 22)

1 cup crumbled queso añejo or feta cheese (4 ounces)

1 cup Mint Vinaigrette (recipe follows)

MINT VINAIGRETTE

❋

MAKES 1 CUP

Place all the ingredients in a medium bowl and whisk together until smooth. Use right away or within a few hours while the mint is still fresh and aromatic.

⅓ cup Fruit Vinegar (page 12) or cider vinegar

1 tablespoon lemon juice

⅔ cup olive oil

1 tablespoon chopped fresh mint leaves

¼ teaspoon salt

¼ teaspoon black pepper

ROMAINE WITH CREAMY ROQUEFORT DRESSING AND CORNMEAL CHILI STRIPS

❈

SERVES 4

LEAFY GREENS ARE COMMON IN THE MEXICAN DIET, BUT THEY'RE ALMOST ALWAYS COOKED. THE EXCEPTIONS ARE AMONG CITY FOLK AND IN UPSCALE **TURISTA** RESTAURANTS WHERE YOU OFTEN FIND A SALAD OF ROMAINE OR SPINACH LEAVES. WHEN SALAD IS SERVED IN MEXICO, IT'S LIKELY TO HAVE A CHEESY, CREAMY DRESSING. THE MOST FAMOUS OF THESE, OF COURSE, IS THE WORLD-RENOWNED CAESAR DRESSING ORIGINALLY FROM CAESAR'S RESTAURANT IN TIJUANA. ELSEWHERE IN MEXICO, YOU FIND AN EQUALLY FAVORED SAUCY ROQUEFORT DRESSING DRIZZLED OVER YOUR ROMAINE LEAVES. I'VE ADDED THE CHILI STRIPS FOR CRUNCH AND A CHANGE FROM THE MORE PROSAIC CROUTONS.

Remove the outer leaves from the lettuces, stripping them down to the light green hearts. Reserve the outer leaves for another dish. Wash and pat dry the hearts, then cut them lengthwise into ¾-inch strips. Place the strips on a platter or individual plates and arrange the tomatoes around them.

Spoon the dressing over the salad, strew the chili strips over the top, and serve right away.

2 heads romaine lettuce

2 small tomatoes, cut into wedges

2 cups Creamy Roquefort Dressing
(recipe follows)

1 cup Cornmeal Chili Strips
(page 108)

CREAMY ROQUEFORT DRESSING

❈

MAKES 2 CUPS

Place all the ingredients in a food processor and mix well. Use right away or store in the refrigerator for up to 2 days.

⅔ cup crumbled Roquefort cheese, at
room temperature (4 ounces)

1 teaspoon chopped fresh oregano leaves
or ½ teaspoon dried oregano

½ cup (packed) chopped chives

½ cup lemon juice

1 cup olive oil

CORNMEAL CHILI STRIPS

✺

MAKES 1 CUP

1 egg

2 tablespoons water

4 large Anaheim or poblano chilies,
   stemmed, seeded, and cut into
   3-by-½- to 4-by-½-inch strips
   (½ pound)

¼ cup cornmeal

¼ cup peanut or other vegetable oil

Salt

Crack the egg into a medium bowl. Add the water and whisk together, mixing well. Add the chili strips and turn to coat all the pieces. Set aside handy to the stove.

Place the cornmeal in another medium bowl. Set aside also handy to the stove.

Heat the oil in a large heavy skillet until it begins to smoke. Transfer half the chili strips to the cornmeal and turn to coat all the pieces. Place the coated strips in the skillet and fry over medium-high heat, stirring, until wilted and golden, about 2 minutes. Transfer to paper towels to drain. Bread and fry the rest of the strips. Salt lightly and use right away, while still crunchy.

BLACK BEAN SALAD

❋

SERVES 6 TO 8

MY LOVE OF FOOD PREPARATIONS THAT KEEP WELL IN THE REFRIGERATOR FOR SEVERAL DAYS, THERE TO GRAZE UPON WHEN HUNGER CALLS BUT TIME IS SHORT, LED ME TO TOSS BLACK BEANS INTO THIS MOST UNTYPICAL SALAD MIXTURE. MEXICAN COOKS MIGHT CALL IT A DRY SOUP; I THINK OF IT AS A BLACK BEAN SALAD. OVER HOT STEAMED RICE, IT'S PERFECT COMFORT FOOD.

Drain the beans, retaining enough of the liquid to keep the beans moist. Reserve the remaining liquid for another dish. Transfer the beans to a large bowl. Add the remaining ingredients and toss to mix. Serve right away or cover and refrigerate for up to 4 days.

1 recipe (6 cups) Pot Beans made with black beans (page 96)

1 jalapeño chili, stemmed and finely chopped

2 small tomatoes, cut into ¼-inch dice

1 small red onion, finely chopped, or 6 scallions, trimmed and minced

½ cup coarsely chopped cilantro leaves

¼ cup fresh lime juice

½ teaspoon salt

CACTUS PADDLE SALAD

✸

SERVES 6

ONE SUNDAY ON A CORNER NEAR THE BUSY TOWN SQUARE IN COYOUACAN, I WAS FASCINATED BY THE ACTIVITY AT A ONE-MAN STAND. THE VENDOR SAT ON A PORTABLE STOOL WITH A PORTABLE TABLE PROPPED IN FRONT OF HIM. HIS KNIFE ALMOST PURRED AS HE DEFTLY SET ABOUT CLEANING AND CUTTING **NOPALES** CACTUS PADDLES. THE AFTER-MASS SHOPPERS WOULD SOON ARRIVE TO BUY THE READY-TO-USE **NOPALES** THEY WOULD TURN INTO SOUP, SALAD, OR PERHAPS PREPARE **EN ESCABECHE** FOR THE LARGE MIDDAY MEAL. MANY CUSTOMERS WERE EXPECTED, IT SEEMED, FROM THE WAY HIS HANDS FLEW OVER THE TASK AND THE AMOUNT HE PILED UP FOR SALE IN SUCH A SHORT TIME. **TURISTAS** THAT DAY, NOT COOKS, WE LONGINGLY ADMIRED HIS NEATLY BAGGED PACKAGES OF PERFECTLY DICED **NOPALES** GLEAMING IN THE SUN AS WE WANDERED OFF TO VIEW THE ART IN THE CHURCH AND MUNCH ON WARM HOMEMADE POTATO CHIPS AND SALSA OFF A CART. WHEN WE PASSED BY AGAIN, HIS TABLE WAS EMPTY. BACK HOME IN OUR OWN KITCHEN, A CACTUS PADDLE SALAD WAS AT THE TOP OF OUR MENU.

4 large cactus paddles (about 1 pound), thorns removed (see Note)

2 quarts water

1 tablespoon salt

3 scallion tops

¼ cup Fruit Vinegar (page 12) or cider vinegar

1 tablespoon fresh lime juice

⅓ cup olive oil

2 teaspoons chopped fresh oregano leaves or 1 teaspoon dried oregano

1 recipe Wilted Red Onions (page 22)

½ cup crumbled queso fresco or feta cheese (2 ounces)

2 canned chipotle chilies, drained and finely chopped

With a paring knife, cut off the bumpy nodes from both sides of the cactus paddles, then pare all around the outer rim. Cut the paddles into 2-by-¼-inch strips.

Place the water, salt, and green onion tops in a large pot and bring to a boil. Drop in the cactus strips and bring back to a boil. Reduce the heat and simmer until tender but not soft, about 10 minutes. Drain the strips, rinse with cool water to wash away the sticky juices, and shake to dry slightly.

When ready to serve the salad, whisk together the vinegar, lime juice, oil, and oregano in a small bowl. Mound the cactus strips on a platter and pour the vinegar mixture over them. Arrange the onions over the top, sprinkle on the cheese and chilies, and serve.

NOTE: The cactus paddles we find in produce markets or supermarkets are usually dethorned. If yours are not, handle them gingerly, perhaps with tongs, and use a paring knife to cut away the thorns, along with the nodes underneath.

CHICKPEA SALAD

✸

SERVES 6

IF YOU EVER HAVE THE GOOD FORTUNE, AS I DID ONCE, TO COME ACROSS FRESHLY PICKED, NOT DRIED, CHICKPEAS, PURCHASE THEM. THE TIME AND EFFORT SPENT PULLING THEM OFF THE STEMS AND HULLING THEM YIELDS A RICH REWARD. SWEET, NUTTY, AND EARTHY, THEY COOK UP SOFT AND TENDER IN HALF THE TIME AS THE DRIED. OTHERWISE, I SUGGEST TAKING THE TIME AND EFFORT TO COOK DRIED CHICKPEAS YOURSELF RATHER THAN USING CANNED ONES. THE LATTER ARE EASY BUT MISS THE MARK BY A MILE.

2 cups dried chickpeas (¾ pound)

1 teaspoon salt

1 large red bell pepper, roasted, peeled, and seeded (page 13), cut into very thin 1-inch strips

3 large garlic cloves, minced or pressed

1 small red onion, finely chopped

¼ cup chopped fresh mint leaves

½ cup chopped fresh parsley leaves

¼ cup fresh lemon juice

½ cup olive oil

Place the chickpeas in a large pot, add water to cover by 1½ inches, and bring to a boil. Remove from the heat and set aside to soak for 1 hour.

Drain the chickpeas and return them to the pot. Add 8 cups of water and bring to a boil. Reduce the heat and simmer until almost tender, 50 minutes to 1 hour and 15 minutes. Stir in ½ teaspoon of the salt and simmer until the chickpeas are very tender, 10 to 15 minutes. Drain, reserving the cooking liquid for another dish, if desired.

Transfer the chickpeas to a large bowl and add the remaining ½ teaspoon salt and the rest of the ingredients. Toss to mix. Serve right away or cover and refrigerate for up to 5 days.

MEXICAN FRIED POTATOES

✦

SERVES 4 TO 6

CONSIDERING THAT POTATOES ARE A NEW WORLD CROP CULTIVATED IN MEXICO SINCE THE SPANISH BROUGHT THEM FROM PERU IN THE SIXTEENTH CENTURY, IT'S STRANGE THAT SIMPLE FRIED POTATOES ARE NOT ALL THAT COMMON IN MEXICAN CUISINE. **PAPAS FRITAS**, AS THEY ARE CALLED, DO SHOW UP AS A TACO TOPPING, BUT USUALLY FRIED POTATOES ARE EMBELLISHED WITH TOMATOES AND CHILI STRIPS. YOU CAN ADD CHEESE AND SALSA TOPPINGS TO THE SIMPLE **PAPAS FRITAS** TO ROUND OUT THE DISH FOR A LIGHT MEAL, OR YOU CAN SCRAMBLE IN A FEW EGGS FOR A HEARTIER PREPARATION. YOU CAN ALSO MAKE THE DISH IN ANY OF ITS VERSIONS WITH SWEET POTATOES.

Heat the oil in a large heavy skillet. Add the potatoes, stir to coat with the oil, then pat into a flat layer. Cook over medium heat until they begin to sizzle and turn golden around the edges, about 10 minutes. Stir in the onion and chili and pat into a flat layer again. Cook over medium heat until the potatoes are browned on the bottom, about 5 minutes. With a spatula, turn the potatoes over to brown the other side.

If using the tomatoes, stir them in and pat into a layer again. Sprinkle with salt to taste, raise the heat to medium-high, and cook until the potatoes are nicely browned on the bottom again, about 5 minutes.

If using the cheese, sprinkle over the top and cook 2 minutes more, or until the cheese softens. Serve right away.

⅓ cup vegetable oil

2 pounds red or white potatoes, scrubbed and cut into ¼-inch dice

1 medium onion, cut into ¼-inch dice

1 poblano or 2 jalapeño chilies, stemmed, seeded, and sliced into very thin strips

2 medium tomatoes, peeled and seeded (page 14), coarsely chopped (½ pound) (optional)

Salt, to taste

1 cup grated Monterey Jack or white cheddar cheese (optional)

MEXICAN POTATO SALAD

✺

SERVES 6

I'VE NEVER MET A POTATO SALAD I DIDN'T LOVE. MUSTARDY, VINEGARY SLICES FROM GERMANY, CUR-RIED CUBES INTERMINGLED WITH OTHER VEGETABLE BITS IN WARM INDIAN **GOBIS**, COLD AND CREAMY MAYONNAISE-COATED CHUNKS FROM CHILDHOOD PICNICS, THEY ALL SATISFY. HERE, IN COMPANY WITH NEW WORLD FLAVORS, POTATOES GET BACK TO THEIR ROOTS.

Put the potatoes in a medium pot, add water to cover by 1 inch, and bring to a boil. Reduce the heat and simmer until the potatoes are soft all the way through but not disintegrating, about 7 minutes. Drain and set aside to cool and dry out a bit, 15 to 20 minutes.

Transfer the potatoes to a large bowl, add the mustard, and toss to coat. Add the remaining ingredients and gently mix. Serve right away at room temperature.

NOTE: Red or white potatoes are the most common varieties used in Mexican cooking, but I prefer to use russet or Idaho potatoes for salads because they cook up soft enough to absorb other flavors yet set up firm enough for salad.

4 medium russet potatoes, peeled or scrubbed, cut into ¼-inch cubes (1 pound)

1 tablespoon Dijon mustard

8 large, Sicilian-type green olives, pitted and coarsely chopped

2 pickled jalapeños, stemmed, seeded, and coarsely chopped (page 13)

12 radishes, trimmed and sliced into thin rounds

4 scallions, trimmed and minced

¾ cup chopped cilantro leaves

2 tablespoons cider vinegar

2 tablespoons olive oil

½ teaspoon salt

½ teaspoon black pepper

SAUTÉED CHILI STRIPS

✺

SERVES 6

IN MEXICAN COOKING, SAUTÉED CHILI STRIPS ARE CALLED **RAJAS**, MEANING SPLINTERS, AFTER THE SPANISH VERB **RAJAR**, TO SLICE. IN COOKING, **RAJAS** MEANS THINLY SLICED ROASTED AND PEELED CHILIES COOKED PLAIN OR FANCY. IN THE PLAINEST VERSION, THE CHILI STRIPS ARE SAUTÉED WITH ONION, NOTHING MORE; THESE **RAJAS** ARE A CLASSIC GARNISH FOR MANY A PLATE. FANCIER VERSIONS, MORE OF A CENTERPIECE TO HEAP OVER RICE OR POTATOES, MIGHT INCLUDE GARLIC, HERBS (THYME, MARJORAM, OREGANO, BAY), AND, SOMETIMES, ROASTED, PEELED, AND SEEDED TOMATOES. PLAIN OR FANCY, **RAJAS** ARE A GOOD DISH TO COOK IN A DOUBLE BATCH. THEY KEEP IN THE REFRIGERATOR FOR UP TO A WEEK AND ARE DELICIOUS HOT OR COLD.

¼ cup vegetable oil

1 large onion, halved and thinly sliced

8 medium poblano chilies, roasted,
*   peeled, and seeded (page 13), cut into*
*   ¼-inch-wide strips (1½ pounds)*

½ teaspoon salt

Heat the oil in a large heavy skillet. Add the onion and sauté over medium heat until soft, about 5 minutes. Stir in the chili strips and salt and sauté until the chilies and onion are very soft, 5 to 6 minutes. Serve right away or cool, cover, and refrigerate for up to 1 week.

MY FAVORITE RAJAS VARIATION

✺

Substitute 4 medium to large red bell peppers for 4 of the poblano chilies, roasted, peeled, seeded, and sliced in the same way. Add 8 garlic cloves, very coarsely chopped, when you wilt the onions. Add 1 teaspoon chopped fresh oregano leaves, 1 crumbled bay leaf, and ¼ cup drained capers when you add the pepper strips. If desired, sprinkle a few drops of fresh lemon juice over the top just before serving. Serve over a mound of White Rice (page 91).

CHAYOTE STEWED WITH TOMATOES, RAISINS, AND WHITE WINE

✺

SERVES 4 TO 6

CHAYOTE, ALSO CALLED "VEGETABLE PEAR," "CHRISTOPHINE," AND "MIRLITON" (IN THE SOUTHERN UNITED STATES), IS NATIVE TO CENTRAL AMERICA AND WIDELY USED IN MEXICAN COOKING. AS A MEMBER OF THE GOURD FAMILY AND A CLOSE RELATIVE OF SUMMER SQUASHES, LIKE SUMMER SQUASHES IT IS INHERENTLY BLAND AND REQUIRES FLAVORFUL INGREDIENTS TO ENHANCE ITS CUCUMBERLIKE, MILD AND WATERY TASTE. UNLIKE SUMMER SQUASHES, HOWEVER, IT DOES NOT QUICKLY DISINTEGRATE BUT REMAINS FIRM WHEN COOKED, SO IT HAS AN ADVANTAGE WHEN STEWED AND STUFFED. THE PEEL OF THE CHAYOTE, ON THE OTHER HAND, MORE CLOSELY RESEMBLES THAT OF THE WINTER SQUASHES. IT DOESN'T TENDERIZE DURING COOKING, SO IT SHOULD BE PARED AWAY, UNLESS YOU ARE USING THE CHAYOTE FOR A STUFFED VEGETABLE DISH WHERE THE PEEL IS NOT EATEN. SOME COOKS ADVISE REMOVING THE LARGE KERNEL IN THE CENTER OF THE CHAYOTE. THEY MUST NOT KNOW THE SECRET OF MEXICAN AND SOUTHERN COOKS: THERE'S NO NEED—IT'S A PRIZE.

Heat the oil in large nonreactive pot. Add the onion, garlic, chili, raisins, and oregano and sauté over medium heat until softened without browning, about 1 minute. Stir in the tomatoes and continue cooking over medium-low heat until the mixture thickens slightly, about 5 minutes more.

Stir in the chayote, wine, and salt, partly cover the pot, and simmer until the chayote is very pale and tender but still a little crunchy and the liquid is saucy, about 25 minutes. Stir from time to time and adjust the heat to prevent over-browning. Sprinkle the parsley over the top. Serve right away.

NOTE: A standard vegetable peeler, the kind you would use for peeling potatoes or carrots, works nicely for peeling chayote.

¼ cup olive oil

1 medium onion, quartered and thinly sliced

2 garlic cloves, minced or pressed

1 serrano chili, stemmed and chopped

2 tablespoons raisins

1 teaspoon chopped fresh oregano leaves or ½ teaspoon dried oregano

3 medium tomatoes, peeled and seeded (page 14), coarsely chopped (¾ pound)

2 large or 3 medium chayote squash, peeled and cut into ½-inch pieces (1½ pounds)

⅔ cup white wine

½ teaspoon salt

2 tablespoons chopped fresh parsley leaves

BRAISED GREENS WITH BLACK OLIVES AND CAPERS

❋

SERVES 4 TO 6

QUELITES WAS THE ANCIENT NAHUATL WORD (AND IT'S USED TO THIS DAY IN MEXICAN SPANISH) TO DESCRIBE THAT ESSENTIAL COMPONENT OF A WHOLESOME DIET BROADLY CATEGORIZED AS LEAFY GREENS. THOUGH GREENS WERE ORIGINALLY FORAGED AND GATHERED FROM THE WILD, MODERN COOKS IN MEXICO, AS HERE, RELY ON MARKET VENDORS FOR THEIR NORMAL SUPPLY OF **QUELITES**. WHETHER FROM FIELD OR MARKET, WHEN THEY ARE STEWED WITH OLIVES, CAPERS, AND FRUITY OLIVE OIL, THE FAINT BITTERNESS OF WILD GREENS, AND ALSO THAT OF SOME CULTIVATED ONES LIKE KALE AND MUSTARD, IS GIVEN A CIVILIZED APPEAL. IF YOUR TASTE RUNS TO THE TRULY TAME, SWISS CHARD AND SPINACH BOTH HAVE A LESS TRENCHANT FLAVOR BUT ARE STILL VERY GOOD AND EQUALLY HEALTHFUL.

2 pounds leafy greens, such as Swiss chard, beet, spinach or young kale, mustard, or dandelion, tough stems removed

3 tablespoons olive oil

1 small onion, finely chopped

1 garlic clove, minced or pressed

1 poblano or 2 jalapeño chilies, stemmed and finely chopped

12 black olives, such as kalamatas, pitted and coarsely chopped

⅓ cup capers, drained

Salt, to taste

Cut the greens crosswise into ½-inch strips and rinse in plenty of cold water. Lift the greens out of the water, transfer to a colander, and set aside to drain.

Heat the oil in a large nonreactive pot. Add the onion, garlic, and chili and sauté until the onion wilts, about 2 minutes. Stir in the greens, olives, and capers. Cover the pot and cook over medium heat until the greens are tender, 8 to 10 minutes.

Season with salt to taste. Serve right away.

STUFFED CHAYOTE WITH PEANUTS AND DRESSED CILANTRO

✸

SERVES 4 TO 6

IF YOU ARE SOMEONE WHO ENJOYS STUFFED VEGETABLES, YOU WILL BE DELIGHTED TO DISCOVER CHAYOTE. THE SAME CHARACTERISTICS THAT MAKE IT IDEAL FOR STEWING ALSO MAKE IT IDEAL FOR STUFFING AND BAKING. CHAYOTE PROVIDES A FIRM EDIBLE CONTAINER TO TRANSPORT A CARGO OF STEAMING SAVORY FILLING TO YOUR PLATE, AND YOU DON'T HAVE TO PEEL THE SQUASH FOR THIS.

*4 medium chayote squash
    (about 2 pounds)*

1½ cups cooked long-grain white rice

1 small onion, finely chopped

2 garlic cloves, minced or pressed

*1 jalapeño chili, stemmed and finely
    chopped*

*1 teaspoon chopped fresh oregano leaves
    or ½ teaspoon dried oregano*

1 tablespoon chopped fresh parsley leaves

½ teaspoon salt

1 medium tomato, finely chopped

2 medium tomatoes, coarsely chopped

1 tablespoon olive oil

½ cup salted roasted peanuts

¼ teaspoon cayenne

½ cup Dressed Cilantro (page 22)

Heat the oven to 350 degrees F. Cut the chayotes in half and scoop out the centers, leaving a ¼-inch shell of the pulp. Coarsely chop the scooped-out pulp. Set aside the squash halves and chopped pulp.

Place the rice, onion, garlic, jalapeño, oregano, parsley, salt, and finely chopped tomato in a bowl and mix together. Spread half the chopped pulp and the coarsely chopped tomatoes in the bottom of a nonreactive baking dish large enough to hold all the squash halves in a single layer. Set the squash halves on top and fill each with the rice mixture, dividing evenly. Spread the remaining half of the chopped pulp over the top. Drizzle the olive oil over all. Pour the water into the dish, carefully so that it doesn't go into the center of any of the squashes, to a depth of about ¼ inch. Cover the dish with a lid or aluminum foil. Bake for 1½ hours, or until the squashes are tender.

Spread the peanuts in an ungreased skillet or on a microwave-safe plate and sprinkle with the cayenne. Stir over medium-high heat or microwave, uncovered, on high until lightly toasted, about 3 minutes. Remove and cool. Coarsely chop.

When the chayotes are cooked, sprinkle the peanuts and dressed cilantro over the top. Serve right away.

CHILES RELLENOS WITH FRESH GREEN CHILIES

✻

SERVES 6

THERE'S NO WAY TO IMPROVE UPON THE CLASSIC STUFFED PEPPERS OF MEXICAN COOKING, SO I DON'T FUSS OR FIDGET WITH THE TRIED AND TRUE. I ALWAYS MAKE THE DISH IN THE TRADITIONAL WAY, AND I INCLUDE THE RECIPE SO YOU CAN, TOO.

Roast the peppers as described on page 13, taking care to remove them from the heat when the skins are charred and blistered but the pulp is still firm. Let cool as usual. Rub the skins off with your fingers, keeping the peppers intact.

Slit each pepper open lengthwise along one side and gently remove the seeds and vein. Spread about ¼ cup cheese in the center of each pepper and press closed. Secure with toothpicks if necessary. Set aside.

Beat the egg whites in a large nonreactive bowl until stiff. Beat in the salt, then the egg yolks, one at a time.

Pour ½ inch of oil into a heavy skillet and heat until almost smoking. Sprinkle flour over as many peppers as will fit into the pan in a single uncrowded layer, then dip each pepper in the egg mixture. Place in the oil and fry until golden on the bottom, turn, and fry until golden on the other side, about 1 minute. Remove the peppers to paper towels to drain. Continue until all the peppers are fried.

Arrange the peppers on a platter or individual plates and top with the sauce. Serve right away.

NOTE: Chiles rellenos are not meant to be crisp. You can keep them warm on a baking sheet lined with paper towels in a warm oven for 30 minutes or so until ready to serve.

12 medium Anaheim or poblano chilies (2 pounds)

1¼ pounds grated Monterey Jack, white cheddar, or Muenster cheese, or a mixture

3 large eggs, separated

⅛ teaspoon salt

Vegetable oil, for frying

⅔ cup flour

2 cups Salsa Ranchera (page 25)

CHILES RELLENOS WITH ANCHO CHILIES AND CHERRY TOMATO SALSA

❁

SERVES 4 TO 6

M Y FIRST ENCOUNTER WITH STUFFED DRIED CHILIES WAS NOT IN THEIR HOMELAND, BUT IN OAKLAND, AT THE TABLE OF CHEF CARLOS MARTINEZ. THOUGH IN MEXICO DRIED CHILIES ARE BATTERED AND FRIED, HE'S PERUVIAN-CALIFORNIAN AND HAS IDEAS OF HIS OWN. HE FILLS THE CHILIES WITH GOAT CHEESE AND STEAMS THEM TO SUPPLENESS WITHOUT ANY OIL. IT'S AN INSPIRED INTERPRETATION. FOR THIS DISH, ANCHO CHILIES ARE A MUST. THEY HAVE THE MOST INHERENT FLAVOR OF THE DRIED CHILIES AND ARE THE ONLY ONES WITH SKINS THAT STEAM SOFT AND FORKABLE.

12 ancho chilies

1 pound soft goat cheese, such as
    Montrachet

¼ cup chopped fresh chives

1½ teaspoons chopped fresh oregano
    leaves or ¾ teaspoon dried oregano

2 cups Cherry Tomato Salsa
    (recipe follows)

Place the chilies in a medium pot, cover with water, and bring to a boil. Remove from the heat and push the chilies into the water so that they are all submerged. Set aside to soften for about 15 minutes.

Lift the chilies out of the pot, reserving the liquid. When cool enough to handle, gently pull off the stems and scoop out the seeds. Try to keep the chilies whole.

Place the cheese, chives, and oregano in a bowl and mash with a fork to mix. Stuff the chilies with the cheese mixture and pinch closed. Arrange the stuffed chilies in a single layer in a microwave-safe dish or steamer basket. Pour the reserved liquid up to ¼ inch into the dish or ¾ inch into the steamer, adding water if necessary. Cover and microwave on high for 5 minutes or steam for 15 minutes, until the chilies puff out and are tender.

Transfer the chilies to a platter or individual plates and surround with the salsa. Serve right away.

NOTE: Choose ancho chilies that are shiny, not too dry, and pliable enough to clean and stuff without crumbling.

CHERRY TOMATO SALSA

✹

MAKES 2 CUPS

2 cups cherry tomatoes, preferably yellow

1 jalapeño chili, stemmed and finely
  chopped

1 tablespoon finely chopped shallot

2 tablespoons chopped fresh chives

2 tablespoons chopped cilantro leaves

¼ teaspoon salt

If you can find them, yellow cherry tomatoes make a particularly dazzling color contrast to the mahogany-red ancho chilies.

Stem the tomatoes and cut them into quarters if they are small or eighths if they are large. Place all the ingredients in a bowl and mix. Use right away or set aside at room temperature for several hours.

VEGETARIAN MIXED GRILL FEAST

✸

SERVES 6

MEXICAN COOKS LOVE TO BARBECUE. BE IT AN INDOOR **COMAL** SET OVER A GAS OR HEARTH FLAME OR AN OUTDOOR GRATE SET OVER AN OPEN FIRE OR A COVERED GROUND PIT FOR LONG, SLOW STEAMING, THE GRILL IS A PROMINENT COOKING TOOL, AND "BARBECUED" A FAVORITE FLAVOR. THERE ARE MANY FAMOUS **BARBACOA** AND **PIBIL** DISHES IN MEXICAN CUISINE, FROM PIT-ROASTED LAMB, GOAT, AND CHICKEN TO FISH GRILLED ON THE BEACH. THERE IS ALSO A STRONG TRADITION OF GRILLED VEGETABLES. THE PEELED PEPPERS AND TOMATOES THAT MAKE UP A LARGE PART OF THE BASIC LEXICON OF MEXICAN CUISINE ARE ALWAYS CHAR-GRILLED FOR EASE OF PREPARATION. GRILLED BABY ONIONS, WHICH ARE LARGER THAN SCALLIONS BUT SMALLER THAN KITCHEN ONIONS, ARE SPRINKLED AT THE LAST MINUTE WITH LIME JUICE. THEY FREQUENTLY PROVIDE THE PUNGENT, TANGY VEGETABLE COUNTERPOINT FOR A **BARBACOA** FEAST OR SERVE AS A SIDE PLATE ON THEIR OWN IN **TAQUERIAS** AND **BOTANAS** CAFES. FOLLOWING THE MODE, WE CAN TAKE OFF FROM THERE AND GRILL A PLENTIFUL ARRAY OF VEGETABLES AND FRUIT FOR A VEGETARIAN FEAST. HERE'S ONE OF MY FAVORITE MIXES.

Prepare a charcoal grill, allowing the coals to burn until ash-covered with some red still glowing through, about 30 to 40 minutes.

Place the chili and bell peppers in the center of the grill rack directly above the coals and cook for 20 to 25 minutes, turning once or twice, until charred all around. Remove and let cool. Peel and seed all the peppers (page 13). Slice into ¼-inch strips and transfer to a kitchen platter. Set aside.

While the peppers char in the center of the grill, arrange the sweet potato slices on the rack around the edges of the fire, not directly over the heat. Grill for 15 to 20 minutes, turning once, until golden on both sides and cooked through. Transfer to the kitchen platter.

Place the onions in the center of the grill with the bulbs facing in and the tops facing out. Place the corn pieces between the onions wherever you find room for them but not directly over the coals. Grill the onions and corn, turning once, until the onions are singed but not burned and the corn is tender, 12 to 15 minutes. When done, transfer the onions and corn to the platter with the other vegetables.

4 medium poblano chilies (½ pound)

2 medium red bell peppers (¾ pound)

3 medium sweet potatoes or yams, scrubbed and cut into ½-inch rounds, lightly coated with oil (1½ pounds)

12 small onions with green tops intact, trimmed (see Note)

4 medium ears corn, husked, silks removed, and cut into 2-inch rounds

½ small pineapple, trimmed and cut into ¼-inch rounds

18 corn tortillas

2 limes, cut into wedges

2 cups Fresh Tomato Salsa (page 24)

When there's room on the grill rack, add the pineapple slices, slightly to the edge of the coals, not directly over them. Cook, turning once, 6 to 8 minutes, or until the slices are somewhat soft and nicely charred but still moist. Transfer to the platter.

Finally, place the tortillas on the grill and lightly toast on both sides, about 4 minutes altogether.

Arrange all the vegetables on a serving platter and pour the collected juices from the kitchen platter over the top. Tuck the lime wedges in and around the vegetables. Serve right away, accompanied by the tortillas and salsa on the side.

NOTES: Trim the onions as you would scallions, cutting off the roots and darker green, tough tops. If you don't have small onions with their tops intact, large scallions, young leeks, or ½-inch-thick slices of red, white, or yellow onions make a fine substitute.

If you are preparing a barbecue feast for many people, plan to cook the food in several rounds. Allow time in between rounds to boost the fire with additional charcoal. Add more charcoal when the heat gets too low and allow 20 minutes or so for the new coals to reach the right temperature before continuing.

chapter six

SWEETS

MEXICAN CONFECTIONS AND HOME-STYLE DESSERTS

❈

ALL THE WORLD HAS A SWEET TOOTH, IT SEEMS, AND MEXICO IS NO EXCEPTION. MEXICAN PEOPLE LOVE SWEETS, AND THEY LIKE THEM VERY SWEET. Pastries and candies are a common snack throughout the day, and there's hardly a corner you turn without coming across a confection for sale. At home, Mexican cooks, as everywhere, often rely on their bakeries, pastry shops, and street vendors to provide the dulcet note at meal's end. When desserts are made at home, they are homey, in appearance and in preparation. They serve, nonetheless, to satisfy the desire for "a touch of sweet" to complete the repast.

RICE PUDDING

✸

SERVES 4 TO 6

AFTER FLAN, RICE PUDDING IS PROBABLY THE MOST POPULAR HOME DESSERT IN MEXICO, AND THERE ARE ALMOST AS MANY PUDDING RECIPES AS THERE ARE HOUSEHOLDS IN THE LAND. SOME INCLUDE A PIECE OF LEMON OR ORANGE RIND FOR FLAVOR AND AROMA. OTHERS ADD ALMOND, EITHER EXTRACT OR NUTS TOASTED AND SPRINKLED OVER THE TOP. ANY KIND OF CANDIED FRUIT OR FRUIT PASTE— CHERRIES, CITRON, GUAVA—CAN REPLACE THE RAISINS OR BE INCLUDED WITH THEM, AS CAN COCONUT SHREDS. PLEASE YOURSELF.

Place the rice and water in a bowl and set aside to soak for 15 minutes. Drain in a colander and rinse with cold water.

Combine the sugar, cinnamon, and milk in a medium saucepan. Bring to a boil and stir in the rice. Reduce the heat, cover, and cook over low heat until the rice is very tender but the mixture is still quite liquid, about 20 minutes. Stir in the raisins, egg yolks, and vanilla. Cook, uncovered, just until the pudding begins to boil again. Remove from the heat right away. Serve warm or chilled.

½ cup long-grain white rice

2 cups warm water

1 cup sugar

2-inch piece cinnamon stick

4 cups milk

½ cup raisins

2 egg yolks, beaten

1 teaspoon vanilla extract

FLAN

✸

SERVES 6

FLAN IS A MOST ACCOMMODATING DESSERT. IT PLEASES THE FRENCH, THE SPANISH, AMERICANS—
NORTH AND SOUTH—THE YOUNG AND THE OLD ALIKE. RESTAURATEURS INCLUDE IT ON THE MENU,
SWEETLY, TO SOOTHE A WIDE RANGE OF CLIENTELE. MANY HOUSEWIVES WHIP ONE UP FOR A QUICK AND
EASY, END-OF-THE-MEAL DELIGHT. AT HOME, DEPENDING ON THE OCCASION, YOU CAN COAT SMALL
RAMEKINS WITH THE CARAMEL AND BAKE INDIVIDUAL PORTIONS TO PRESENT AS IS OR UNMOLDED AND
INVERTED TO SHOW OFF THE CARAMEL AND YOUR EXPERTISE. MOST EASILY, YOU CAN MAKE A FAMILY
AFFAIR OF IT. BAKE THE FLAN IN A LARGE DISH AND SERVE IT WITHOUT UNMOLDING, JUST SPOONING
THE CARAMEL FROM THE BOTTOM AS YOU SCOOP UP THE CUSTARD.

1 cup sugar

1 tablespoon water

4 cups milk

2-inch piece cinnamon stick

2-inch piece lemon peel

4 large eggs

1 egg yolk

1 teaspoon vanilla extract

Heat the oven to 325 degrees F. Place ½ cup of the sugar and the water in a heavy
skillet. Place over medium-high heat and stir occasionally until the sugar melts.
Reduce the heat to medium and cook, stirring from time to time, until bubbles
break from the bottom of the pan and the mixture is caramel-colored, about
3 minutes.

Pour the caramel mixture into a 1½-quart glass or ceramic baking dish (or
divide it among 6 ramekins or custard cups). Tilt to spread the caramel evenly
over the bottom and up the sides a little (it will stick and harden as it cools).
Set aside.

Combine the milk, cinnamon, lemon peel, and remaining ½ cup of sugar in a
large saucepan. Bring to a boil, reduce the heat, and simmer for 2 minutes to
reduce slightly. (Watch the pot as the milk comes to a boil; it can rapidly over-
flow.) Remove from the heat and set aside to cool.

Crack the eggs into a bowl. Add the yolk and vanilla and beat until frothy.
Pour the milk through a strainer into the eggs, discarding the cinnamon stick and
lemon peel, and beat to mix. Pour the egg and milk mixture into the dish with
the caramel.

Place the flan dish in a larger baking dish. Add water to the larger dish to
come half way up the sides of the smaller dish. Cover with aluminum foil and
place in the oven. Bake until a knife inserted in the center of the flan comes out

clean, about 45 minutes (or 30 minutes for ramekins). Remove and let cool in the water bath at room temperature for several hours before serving.

When ready to serve, remove the flan from the water bath. Place a serving dish over the baking dish. Holding them together, turn them over to invert the flan. It should drop out of the baking dish onto the platter. If not, set the flan dish in a hot-water bath for a few seconds to loosen it, then invert again. Serve right away.

DESSERT EMPANADAS

✸

MAKES TWELVE 6-INCH EMPANADAS

SUGAR-DUSTED DEEP-FRIED FRITTERS SPEAK TO MANY A TONGUE. BEIGNETS, DONUTS, **CHURROS**, SOPAIPILLAS, OR DESSERT EMPANADAS, ALL ARE WARM, SWEET, AND FRANKLY, FAT LADEN. THEY ARE AN INDULGENCE, THOUGH THESE EMPANADAS CAN BE BAKED TO AVOID SOME OF THE FAT AND SATISFY A CRAVING IN A MODIFIED WAY (SEE NOTE).

1 recipe Empanada Dough (page 60)

2 cups Apple and Pecan Empanada Filling (recipe follows)

Vegetable oil, for frying

½ cup powdered sugar

1 egg yolk whisked with 1 tablespoon water (optional)

Make and roll out the dough as described on page 60.

Place a scant 2 tablespoons of the apple filling in the center of each circle and fold the dough over to make a half-moon. Moisten the outer edge of the dough with water and press all around the edge with the tines of a fork to seal. Cook right away or cover with plastic wrap and refrigerate overnight.

When ready to cook the empanadas, pour oil to a depth of 1 inch into a heavy saucepan or deep skillet. Heat the oil until it sizzles when you splash a drop of water in it (about 375 degrees F.) Add as many empanadas as will fit in a single uncrowded layer and fry, turning once, until golden on both sides, about 5 minutes. Transfer to paper towels to drain. Continue until all the empanadas are fried, bringing the oil back to 375 degrees F. between batches.

While the empanadas are still warm, dust with powdered sugar, sifted through a strainer. Serve right away or within several hours.

NOTE: To bake the empanadas, preheat the oven to 425 degrees F. Place the empanadas on an ungreased baking sheet and brush the tops with the egg yolk mixture. Bake until the tops are golden, the edges lightly browned, and the dough is cooked all the way through, 20 to 25 minutes. Dust with powdered sugar and serve warm.

APPLE AND PECAN EMPANADA FILLING

✹

MAKES 2 CUPS

Melt the butter in a medium skillet over medium-high heat. Add the pecans and stir until lightly toasted, about 2 minutes. Add the apples, raisins, sugar, cinnamon, cloves, and lime juice and stir to mix. Cover and simmer until the apples are very soft, about 15 minutes. Remove and cool. Use when cool or refrigerate overnight.

4 tablespoons butter

¼ cup pecans, finely chopped

2 large firm-fleshed, slightly tart apples, such as Granny Smith, Pippin, or Gala, peeled, cored, and finely chopped (1 pound)

¼ cup raisins

¼ cup sugar

½ teaspoon ground cinnamon

⅛ teaspoon ground cloves

3 tablespoons lime juice

SWEET NUT TAMALES WITH STRAWBERRY MANGO SAUCE

✹

MAKES 20 TAMALES

"**H**OT" TAMALES ARE THE ONES YOU FIND IN RESTAURANTS AND TAKE-OUT STANDS. SWEET TAMALES ARE THE ONES YOU FIND AT HOME. MADE OF **MASA** DOUGH LIKE THEIR SAVORY COUNTERPARTS, SWEET TAMALES ARE A QUINTESSENTIAL NEW WORLD DESSERT. IN PRE-HISPANIC TIMES, THEY WERE PROBABLY SWEETENED WITH HONEY AND FILLED OR TOPPED WITH A NUT OR FRUIT PUREE. TODAY, WE EXCHANGE THE MORE SUBTLE SWEETNESS OF HONEY FOR SUGAR AND KEEP THE NUTRITIOUS CORN, NUTS, AND FRUIT.

Sweet Tamale Dough

2 cups masa harina

1 teaspoon baking powder

½ cup sugar

¼ teaspoon salt

8 tablespoons (1 stick) butter or ½ cup
    vegetable oil

1½ cups milk or water

30 to 50 dried corn husks, soaked to
    soften (page 64), or about twice as
    many fresh corn husks, rinsed

1 cup Nut Filling for Sweet Tamales
    (page 138)

2 cups Strawberry Mango Sauce
    (page 138)

1 cup Homemade Thickened Cream
    (page 41)

Combine the *masa harina,* baking powder, sugar, and salt in a medium bowl and stir with a fork to mix well. Set aside.

Place the butter in a large bowl and beat until light and fluffy. Alternately beat in the *masa* mixture and milk ½ cup at a time to make a moist batter.

Following the directions on pages 64–65, set up a steamer and bring the water to a boil. Form the tamales, spreading about 2 scant teaspoons of the nut filling in the center of each corn husk. Arrange the tamales seam side down in the steamer. Steam as described for 1 hour, or until the dough pulls away from the husks, is no longer moist and sticky, and is cooked through.

Serve the tamales warm or at room temperature, topped with the sauce and the cream.

NUT FILLING
FOR SWEET TAMALES

❋

MAKES 1 CUP

1 cup pecans, walnuts, pine nuts,
   blanched almonds, or a mixture
2 tablespoons sugar
¼ teaspoon ground cinnamon
2 tablespoons butter

Place all the ingredients in a food processor and process as fine as possible. Use right away or transfer to a bowl, cover, and refrigerate for up to several days.

STRAWBERRY MANGO SAUCE

❋

MAKES 2 CUPS

1 cup strawberries, hulled and coarsely
   chopped
1 mango, peeled, pitted, and coarsely
   chopped
1 tablespoon sugar
1 tablespoon tequila

As well as topping dessert tamales, this strawberry sauce can make a rice pudding or scoop of vanilla ice cream special. It's best served the same day.

Place all the ingredients in a medium nonreactive pot. Bring to a boil, reduce the heat, and simmer until slightly thickened but still brightly colored, about 15 minutes. Use right away or set aside at room temperature for up to several hours.

MEXICAN BREAD PUDDING

✲

SERVES 6

ISHES THAT SUCCEED IN MAKING "A SILK PURSE OUT OF A SOW'S EAR" ARE SOME OF MY PERSONAL FAVORITES. MEXICAN BREAD PUDDING, CALLED **CAPIROTADA**, IS SUCH A ONE. IT ECONOMIZES ON OLD BUT NOT FORGOTTEN BREAD FOR **DESSERT**. WITH NO EGGS OR MILK TO MAKE A CUSTARD, IT'S NOT REALLY A PUDDING. WITH LOTS OF SUGAR TO CARAMELIZE THE BREAD CUBES, IT'S A BREAD CANDY. A VERY THRIFTY CANDY IS WHAT IT IS.

Heat the oven to 350 degrees F. Spread the bread cubes and nuts in a single layer on a baking sheet. Place in the oven and toast lightly without browning, about 8 minutes. Set aside to cool.

Place the sugar, cinnamon, cloves, butter, and water in a medium pot. Bring to a boil, reduce the heat, and simmer until the mixture is syrupy, about 15 minutes. Remove from the heat and set aside.

Place the bread, nuts, raisins, cheese, and apples, if using, in a large baking pan and toss to mix. Pour the syrup through a strainer into the dish and stir to mix. Bake until golden on top, about 25 minutes. Serve hot or cold.

NOTE: If you're using bread that's drier and harder than day-old bread, you don't need to toast it. Cut it into ¾-inch chunks and use it straightaway. Toast the nuts separately on the stove top, in the oven, or in the microwave.

½ pound day-old French bread, cut into ¾-inch cubes (see Note)

1 cup pecans, walnuts, peanuts, almonds, or pine nuts, very coarsely chopped

2 cups (packed) dark brown sugar

2-inch piece cinnamon stick

2 whole cloves

4 tablespoons (½ stick) butter

4 cups water

1 cup raisins

2 cups grated Monterey Jack cheese (6 ounces)

2 baking apples, such as Delicious or Granny Smith, peeled, quartered, cored, and sliced ¼ inch thick (optional)

COCONUT CUSTARD

✸

SERVES 4 TO 6

A S WITH MEXICAN BREAD PUDDING, MEXICAN COCONUT CUSTARD, CALLED **COCADA**, HAS DEFINITE TRACES OF CANDY IN ITS TEXTURE AND TASTE. THIS IS AN ADVANTAGE FOR THE BUSY COOK: THE HEAVY SUGAR-SYRUP BASE PREVENTS THE EGG YOLKS FROM CURDLING AS THE CUSTARD SIMMERS. DENSE, SWEET, AND GOOEY, A LITTLE BIT GOES A LONG WAY.

1 cup sugar

1 cup water

2 cups coconut flakes, preferably
*   unsweetened (2 ounces)*

2 tablespoons oloroso sherry (optional)

4 egg yolks

1 cup milk

⅓ cup slivered almonds (1½ ounces)

Combine the sugar and water in a large heavy pot. Bring to a boil and stir in the coconut. Reduce the heat and simmer until the liquid is syrupy and the coconut has turned from transparent back to milky, about 20 minutes. If using the sherry, stir it in and simmer 3 minutes more.

Beat the egg yolks with the milk in a medium bowl. Whisk in about ½ cup of the coconut mixture, then stir the entire egg and coconut mixture into the pot. Cook over medium heat, stirring frequently, until the mixture is thick and custardlike and tiny bubbles break over the entire surface. Transfer to a glass or ceramic dish and set aside to cool and set.

Spread the almonds in an ungreased small skillet or on a microwave-safe plate. Stir over medium-high heat or microwave on high for 4 minutes, until toasted. Sprinkle the almonds over the top of the custard. Serve at room temperature, chilled, or browned for a few minutes in a hot oven or under the broiler.

CANDIED GOURD SQUASH

✸

SERVES 6 TO 8

GOURD SQUASHES PROVIDE A MULTIPLE GLORY FOR THE HOUSEHOLD. BESIDES THE MORE FAMILIAR PREPARATIONS, YOU CAN ALSO CANDY THE PULP FOR A SWEET TREAT. FOR THIS, IT'S NICE TO MIX SEVERAL VARIETIES WHICH PRACTICALLY PUREE THEMSELVES, SUCH AS ACORN OR PUMPKIN, WITH BANANA OR HUBBARD, WHICH RETAIN THEIR SHAPE IN COOKING. IN KEEPING WITH THE STYLE OF MEXICAN SWEETS, CANDIED SQUASH IS NOT A LIGHT DESSERT; **DULCE** IT IS.

2½ to 3 pounds mixed winter squashes, such as pumpkin, acorn, Hubbard, and banana
2 tablespoons sesame seeds
1 cup honey
½ cup sherry
2 cups Homemade Thickened Cream (page 41)

Cut the squashes in half and scoop out the seeds. Set the seeds aside to toast for snacking (page 14). Cut the squash halves lengthwise into 1-inch-wide wedges. Pare off the rind with a knife or vegetable peeler. Slice the wedges crosswise into ¼-inch-thick chunks and set aside.

Put the sesame seeds in an ungreased small skillet or spread on a microwave-safe plate. Stir over medium-high heat or microwave on high until popping and toasted, about 4 minutes. Set aside.

Place the honey and sherry in a large nonreactive pot and bring to a boil. Reduce the heat and simmer until thick enough to coat a spoon, about 10 minutes. Stir in the squash pieces and the sesame seeds. Bring back to a boil, reduce the heat, and simmer until most of the liquid is absorbed and evaporated but the mixture is still moist with a jamlike consistency, 15 to 20 minutes, depending on the type of squash.

Serve right away while still warm or set aside at room temperature for up to several hours. Top with cream just before serving.

NOTE: You can also use candied squash, without the cream topping, to spoon over ice cream or sponge cake, to serve with mixed grills or roasts, or wherever else you might want a sweet condiment.

NUT BRITTLES

✹

MAKES 1½ POUNDS

UNLESS YOU MUST HAVE CHOCOLATE, NUT BRITTLES ARE THE CANDY TO DIE FOR. JUDGING FROM THE AVAILABILITY OF NUT BRITTLES AT STREET STANDS, THE MEXICAN PEOPLE SHARE MY PASSION FOR THEM, AND NOWHERE ON EARTH WILL YOU FIND A FINER VERSION. PECANS, PUMPKIN SEEDS, OR PEANUTS ARE TIGHTLY PACKED, ONE ALMOST ATOP THE OTHER, IN A SWEET SUSPENSION OF CRUNCHY, CHEWABLE BUT NOT TOOTH-BREAKING, CANDY. THE SECRET INGREDIENT IS THE BAKING SODA. IT TURNS THE CANDY CREAMY GOLDEN AND SOFTLY CRACKLY. IT ALSO PROVIDES THE SALTY COUNTER-POINT THAT MAKES YOU KEEP EATING, AND EATING, AND EATING . . .

Combine the sugar, corn syrup, butter, salt, and water in a large nonreactive pot. Bring to a boil. Whisk to dissolve the sugar, reduce the heat, and cook gently until the mixture reaches the soft ball stage (234 to 240 degrees F. on a candy thermometer), about 20 minutes. Stir in the nuts and simmer until the hard crack stage (290 to 300 degrees F.), about 15 minutes. Add the baking soda and whisk briefly until the bubbling stops and the mixture settles. Set aside.

Grease a 16-inch length of heavy-duty aluminum foil with butter. Pour the candy mixture onto the foil and spread ¼ inch thick with a wooden spoon. Let set for at least 20 minutes, then break into pieces. The brittle can be stored in an airtight container at room temperature for up to several weeks.

NOTES: If using salted roasted peanuts, you might want to omit the salt in the recipe, though I don't.

If you don't have a candy thermometer, you can gauge the soft ball stage by drizzling a few drops of the candy mixture into a cup of cool water. If it forms strings that you can easily prod into a ball, it's at the soft ball stage. If it splays out and disintegrates in the water, it's not cooked enough yet. If it tightly balls up as it sinks to the bottom, you've overdone it.

Heavy-duty aluminum foil is a must for candy-making. The thin stuff doesn't hold up.

2 cups sugar

1 cup light corn syrup

2 tablespoons butter

¼ teaspoon salt

¼ cup water

1½ cups pecans, unsalted roasted pumpkin seeds, or salted roasted peanuts (about 6 ounces) (see Note)

½ teaspoon baking soda

MEXICAN CHOCOLATE CHILI COOKIES

✸

MAKES ABOUT 12 DOZEN COOKIES

EVERY OTHER YEAR, MY FRIEND KAREN FRERICHS AND I MAKE COOKIES FOR CHRISTMAS PRESENTS. WE CLAIM THE TIME AND APPOINT THE DATE, NO SCHEDULE INTERFERENCES ALLOWED. WE COLLECT THE INGREDIENTS—YOU HAVE THIS, I HAVE THAT, WE NEED TO SHOP FOR SUCH AND SUCH—AND SPEND THE ENTIRE DAY, DAWN TO DUSK, BAKING AND CONSIDERING OUR NOTES ON PAST BEST COOKIES. FOR A WHILE WE SETTLED ON BISCOTTI, BISCOTTI VARIATIONS, AND SOMETIMES PFEFFERNUSSES. LAST TIME, KAREN BROUGHT A WHOLE NEW CONCEPT TO THE PARTY: MEXICAN CHOCOLATE COOKIES. SHE HAD MADE A BATCH IN ADVANCE FOR A PRE-COOKIE-BAKING TASTE OF COOKIES! THEY WERE DIVINE. I'VE SINCE ADDED CHILI POWDER AND MEXICAN CHOCOLATE TO MY RENDITION. NEXT COOKIE-BAKING YEAR, WE'LL COMPARE NOTES AND ALL OUR FRIENDS AND RELATIVES WILL PROBABLY GET MEXICAN CHOCOLATE COOKIES FOR THE HOLIDAYS. AND MAYBE SOME LIME AND CORNMEAL ONES (PAGE 147), TOO, SINCE WE'RE ON A NEW ROLL HERE.

3 disks Mexican chocolate (9 ounces)

¼ cup water

4 cups flour

½ cup cocoa

2 teaspoons pure chili powder, preferably ancho

1 teaspoon ground cinnamon

¼ teaspoon cayenne

¼ teaspoon salt

12 tablespoons (1½ sticks) butter, at room temperature

1½ cups sugar

1 tablespoon vanilla extract

2 eggs

½ cup powdered sugar

Combine the chocolate disks and water in a small nonreactive saucepan and stir over low heat until the chocolate melts, about 2 minutes. Set aside.

Sift together the flour, cocoa, chili powder, cinnamon, cayenne, and salt. Set aside.

Beat together the butter, sugar, and vanilla in a large bowl until well mixed. Beat in the eggs, then the chocolate. Add the dry ingredient mixture in 2 or 3 batches, beating well after each addition, to make a somewhat moist dough.

Divide the dough into 4 equal parts. On a lightly floured surface, roll each into a log approximately 12 by 1½ inches. Place the dough logs on a sheet of wax paper, cover loosely with another sheet of wax paper, and refrigerate until firm but not hard, 1½ to 2 hours.

When ready to bake the cookies, preheat the oven to 350 degrees F. Slice the dough logs into ¼-inch-thick rounds and arrange on ungreased baking sheets. Bake until light brown and crusty around the edges, 6 minutes. Turn the cookies over and bake until no longer moist in the centers, 8 minutes. Remove from the oven and let cool on the baking sheets for 5 minutes.

Transfer the cookies to a serving platter and sift the powdered sugar over the tops. Serve right away or store in an airtight container for up to 1 week.

NOTE: As with all refrigerator cookies, the important part is not to rush. If you intend to bake the cookies right away, allow at least 1½ to 2 hours lead time; otherwise, the dough will not be properly set. On the other hand, you can make the dough in advance, wrap it well, and refrigerate it for up to several days or freeze it for even longer. Remember, when you remove the dough logs from the refrigerator or freezer, leave them at room temperature until they're soft enough to slice easily.

WEDDING COOKIES

✸

IN THE ELABORATE AND EXTENSIVE PREPARATIONS SURROUNDING A MARRIAGE, THE GIVING AND RECEIVING OF GIFTS PLAYS A MAJOR RITUAL ROLE. FOR THE BRIDE'S PART, SHE ACCEPTS THE CONGRATULATIONS AND COLLECTS THE GIFTS. IN RETURN, AT THE WEDDING CELEBRATION, SHE OFFERS SWEETS TO THE GUESTS, FAMILY AND FRIENDS, TO THANK THEM FOR SHARING HER JOY AND HELPING TO PROVIDE FOR HER FUTURE HOUSEHOLD. WEDDING COOKIES, ALSO CALLED BRIDE'S COOKIES, ARE TRADITIONAL IN MEXICO. YOU CAN HALVE, DOUBLE, OR TRIPLE THE RECIPE, DEPENDING ON THE SIZE OF YOUR PARTY.

1 cup pecans (4 ounces)

½ pound (2 sticks) butter, softened to room temperature

2 cups powdered sugar

1 teaspoon vanilla extract

2¼ cups unbleached all-purpose flour

Using a food processor, chop the pecans as fine as possible. Set aside.

Beat the butter in a large bowl until smooth and fluffy. Beat in ½ cup of the sugar and the vanilla. Add the flour in 3 or 4 batches, beating well after each addition. Stir in the pecans to make a dry dough.

Divide the dough into about 40 large, walnut-size balls. Arrange the balls ¼ inch apart on ungreased baking sheets, cover with plastic wrap, and set aside in the refrigerator to chill until the dough is firm but not hard, about 1½ hours.

When ready to bake the cookies, preheat the oven to 375 degrees F. Bake until the edges of the cookies are beginning to brown, about 12 minutes. Remove from the oven and let cool on the baking sheets until the cookies are cool enough to handle, about 15 minutes.

Sift the remaining 1½ cups sugar onto a plate. Roll each cookie ball in the sugar to coat thoroughly all around. Serve right away or store in an airtight container for up to 1 week.

LIME CORNMEAL COOKIES

✺

MAKES ABOUT 60 COOKIES

YOU MAY HAVE HEARD OF CORNMEAL CRUST FOR PIZZA OR CORNMEAL BREADING FOR CHILI STRIPS, BUT THE CONTENT OF COOKIES? JUST THINK OF DESSERT TAMALES; CORN MAKES A DELIGHTFUL SWEET DOUGH. LACED WITH LIME AND BAKED INTO COOKIES, IT TURNS PLEASINGLY CRUNCHY. LIME CORNMEAL COOKIES ARE OUTSTANDING ENOUGH TO FESTOON A POACHED OR ICED FRUIT DESSERT OR OFFER ALONE.

Place the butter and sugar in a large bowl and beat together. Add the egg, lime juice, orange and lime peels, and almond extract and beat until well mixed. Add the cornmeal and flour and beat until well mixed.

Transfer the dough to a counter liberally sprinkled with flour and cornmeal. Roll the dough around until you can gather it into a neat ball without it sticking to the counter. Wrap in plastic wrap and refrigerate until firm but still malleable, 30 to 45 minutes.

When ready to bake the cookies, preheat the oven to 350 degrees F. Lightly butter baking sheets and sprinkle them lightly with cornmeal. Pinch off walnut-size pieces of the dough and roll them between your palms to make balls. Press each ball to flatten it slightly and place ½ inch apart on the baking sheets. Bake until the cookies start to crack across the top and turn golden on the bottom, about 10 minutes. (Use a spatula to peek under.) Turn the cookies over and bake until golden all around, about 5 minutes. Remove from the oven and let cool on the baking sheets for 5 minutes.

Transfer to a platter. While the cookies are still warm, sift the powdered sugar over the tops. Turn them over to coat with sugar on the other sides. Serve right away or store in an airtight container for up to 1 week.

½ pound (2 sticks) butter, at room
    temperature
1 cup sugar
1 large egg
2 tablespoons fresh lime juice
4 teaspoons finely chopped orange peel
2 teaspoons finely chopped lime peel
1 teaspoon almond extract
1 cup yellow cornmeal
1½ cups unbleached all-purpose flour
½ cup powdered sugar

FRUIT ICE

✹

MAKES 4 CUPS

EVERYWHERE YOU GO IN MEXICO, YOU FIND VENDORS PROFFERING FRESH FRUIT, FROM THE MUN-DANE TO THE PARADISIACAL. THE FRUIT MAY BE PEELED, SLICED, AND READY-TO-EAT; PUREED AND STIRRED WITH MINERAL WATER FOR LIQUID REFRESHMENT; OR POURED OVER CRUSHED ICE AND SERVED AS A SLUSH IN A WAX-PAPER CONE. WHATEVER THE FORM, THE BASIC NOTION IS ESSENCE OF FRUIT. FROZEN INTO A SORBET, FRUIT PUREE BECOMES THE CHILLY, FRAGRANT MOUND AROUND WHICH TO HEAP AN ASSORTMENT OF MEXICAN COOKIES — DESSERT PERFECTION!

4 pounds ripe watermelon, cantaloupe, or other sweet melon, seeded and rind removed, or 6 cups berries, stemmed if necessary, or 6 ripe mangos, peeled and pulp cut off the seeds

⅓ to ⅔ cup superfine sugar, depending on the sweetness of the fruit

3 tablespoons tequila (optional, see Note)

Puree the fruit in a food processor. Transfer the puree to a large bowl. Stir in sugar to taste and the tequila, if using. Mix well to dissolve the sugar. Place the mixture in the freezer and chill until it begins to freeze around the edges and across the top, about 2 hours.

Whisk to break up and mix in the ice crystals, then return to the freezer and chill for 2 hours more.

Whisk again, breaking up the ice crystals and remixing into an evenly granulated mixture. Cover with plastic wrap and return to the freezer until frozen through, 2 to 3 hours more or up to several days.

Remove from the freezer 45 minutes before serving so the ice softens enough to spoon it out.

NOTE: Tequila does more than add flavor. The alcohol prevents the mixture from freezing so solid that you can't spoon it out without completely defrosting it.

INDEX

Achiote, 12

Apples
  Apple and Pecan Empanada Filling, 135
  Dessert Empanadas, 134

Avocados
  Avocado Vichyssoise, 79
  Guacamole, 20

Beans
  Bean Cakes, 99
  Black Bean and Plantain Tamale Filling, 65
  Black Bean Salad, 109
  cooking, 96
  Fava Bean Stew, 100
  lima, 90
  Pot Beans, 96
  refried, 97
  Well-fried Beans with Cheese and Fresh Red Chilies, 97

Bell peppers
  Corn and Sweet Red Pepper Salsa, 36
  My Favorite *Rajas* Variation (Sautéed Chili Strips), 116
  preparing, 13

Black Bean and Plantain Tamale Filling, 65

Black Bean Salad, 109

Braised Greens with Black Olives and Capers, 118

Bread Pudding, Mexican, 139

Cabbage, Shredded, 23

Cactus Paddle Salad, 110

Candied Gourd Squash, 141

Cantaloupes
  Melon and Potato Soup, 78
  Melon Jalapeño Salsa, 34

Capirotada, 139

Carrots and Jalapeños, Pickled, 40

Chayote squash
  about, 117
  Chayote Stewed with Tomatoes, Raisins, and White Wine, 117

Stuffed Chayote with Peanuts and Dressed Cilantro, 120

Cheese
  Chilaquiles, 59
  Chiles con Queso, 50
  Chiles Rellenos with Ancho Chilies and Cherry Tomato Salsa, 122
  Chiles Rellenos with Fresh Green Chilies, 121
  Creamed Corn and Cheese Tamale Filling, 65
  Creamy Roquefort Dressing, 107
  Green Enchiladas in Mole Verde, 55
  Macaroni and Cheese Mexican-Style, 88
  Nachos, 54
  Quesadillas, 5
  Red Enchiladas, 56
  Spinach Salad with Pine Nuts, Cheese, and Mint Vinaigrette, 105
  Well-fried Beans with Cheese and Fresh Red Chilies, 97

Cherry Tomato Salsa, 124

Chickpeas
  Chickpea Salad, 112
  cooking, 112
  Empanadas, 60
  Savory Chickpea and Walnut Empanada Filling, 61

Chilaquiles, 59

Chiles con Queso, 50

Chiles Rellenos with Ancho Chilies and Cherry Tomato Salsa, 122

Chiles Rellenos with Fresh Green Chilies, 121

Chilies
  about, 8, 10–11
  Chiles con Queso, 50
  Chiles Rellenos with Ancho Chilies and Cherry Tomato Salsa, 122
  Chiles Rellenos with Fresh Green Chilies, 121
  Cornmeal Chili Strips, 108
  Melon Jalapeño Salsa, 34
  My Favorite *Rajas* Variation (Sauteed Chili Strips), 116
  Pickled Carrots and Jalapeños, 40
  Piquant Sauce with Chipotle Chilies and Tamarind, 30

preparing, 13
Rajas, 116
Red Enchilada Sauce, 57
Roasted and Marinated Chili Strips, 37
Sautéed Chili Strips, 116
Spaghetti with Spinach, Chilies, Cream, and Almonds, 85
Vermicelli with Tomatoes and Chipotle Chilies, 87
Well-fried Beans with Cheese and Fresh Red Chilies, 97
Chili Salt, 19
Chocolate Chili Cookies, Mexican, 144–45
Chowders. *See* Soups and chowders
Cilantro
Cooked Green Salsa, 29
Dressed Cilantro, 22
Fresh Tomatillo Salsa, 28
Cocada, 140
Coconut Custard, 140
Cooked Green Salsa, 29
Cookies
Lime Cornmeal Cookies, 147
Mexican Chocolate Chili Cookies, 144–45
Wedding Cookies, 146
Corn
about, 11
Corn and Sweet Red Pepper Salsa, 36
Corn Chowder, 74
Corn Tortillas, 45
Creamed Corn and Cheese Tamale Filling, 65
Green *Pozole,* 75
Mexican Polenta, 95
Cornmeal
about, 11
Cornmeal Chili Strips, 108
Lime Cornmeal Cookies, 147
Mexican Polenta, 95
Cream, Homemade Thickened, 41
Creamed Corn and Cheese Tamale Filling, 65
Creamy Roquefort Dressing, 107
Custard
Coconut Custard, 140
Flan, 132

Desserts
Candied Gourd Squash, 141
Coconut Custard, 140
Dessert Empanadas, 134
Flan, 132
Fruit Ice, 148
Lime Cornmeal Cookies, 147
Mexican Bread Pudding, 139
Mexican Chocolate Chili Cookies, 144–45
Nut Brittles, 141
Rice Pudding, 131
Sweet Nut Tamales with Strawberry Mango Sauce, 136
Wedding Cookies, 146
Dressed Cilantro, 22

Empanadas
Apple and Pecan Empanada Filling, 135
Dessert Empanadas, 134
Empanada Dough, 60
Savory Chickpea and Walnut Empanada Filling, 61
Savory Empanadas, 60
Enchiladas
Green Enchiladas in Mole Verde, 55
Red Enchiladas, 56

Fava Bean Stew, 100
Flan, 132
Flour Tortillas, 48
Fresh Tomato Salsa, 24
Fruit Ice, 148
Fruit Vinegar, 12–13

Garlic Soup, Toasted, 72
Golden Rice, 92
Grapefruit and Pumpkin Seed Salsa, 35
Green Enchiladas in Mole Verde, 55
Green *Pozole,* 75
Greens with Black Olives and Capers, Braised, 118
Guacamole, 20

Herbs, 11
Homemade Thickened Cream, 41

Ingredients, 8–14

Jícama and Watermelon Salsa, 33

Lentil and Chard Soup, 71
Lettuce, Shredded, 23
Lima beans, 90
Limes
  as garnish, 23
  Lime Cornmeal Cookies, 147

Macaroni and Cheese Mexican-Style, 88
Mango Sauce, Strawberry, 138
Masa harina, 11
Melon and Potato Soup, 78
Melon Jalapeño Salsa, 34
Mexican Bread Pudding, 139
Mexican Chocolate Chili Cookies, 144–45
Mexican Crudités, 22–23
Mexican Fried Potatoes, 113
Mexican Gazpacho, 81
Mexican Pilaf, 94
Mexican Polenta, 95
Mexican Potato Salad, 115
Mexican Rice, 93
Mint Vinaigrette, 105
Mole Verde, 55
My Favorite *Rajas* Variation (Sautéed Chili Strips), 116

Nachos, 54
Nuts. *See also* individual nuts
  about, 12
  Nut Brittles, 141
  Nut Filling for Sweet Tamales, 138
  Sweet Nut Tamales with Strawberry Mango Sauce, 136
  toasting, 14

Oils, 12
Onions, Wilted Red, 22

Papas fritas, 113
Papaya and Peanut Salsa, 35

Pasta
  Macaroni and Cheese Mexican-Style, 88
  Mexican Pilaf, 94
  Spaghetti a la Primavera Mexicana, 90
  Spaghetti with Spinach, Chilies, Cream, and Almonds, 85
  Vermicelli with Tomatoes and Chipotle Chilies, 87
Peanut Salsa, Papaya and, 35
Pecans
  Apple and Pecan Empanada Filling, 135
  Dessert Empanadas, 134
  Mexican Pilaf, 94
  Wedding Cookies, 146
Peppers. *See* Bell peppers; Chilies
Pickled Carrots and Jalapeños, 40
Pickled Mixed Vegetables, 38
Piquant Sauce with Chipotle Chilies and Tamarind, 30
Plantain Tamale Filling, Black Bean and, 65
Polenta, Mexican, 95
Potatoes
  Avocado Vichyssoise, 79
  Melon and Potato Soup, 78
  Mexican Fried Potatoes, 113
  Mexican Potato Salad, 115
Pot Beans, 96
Pozole, Green, 75
Puddings
  Mexican Bread Pudding, 139
  Rice Pudding, 131
Pumpkin seeds
  Grapefruit and Pumpkin Seed Salsa, 35
  Mole Verde, 55
  Toasted Pumpkin Seeds, 21

Quesadillas, 52

Radishes, 23
Rajas, 116
Red Enchiladas, 56
Red Enchilada Sauce, 57
Refried beans, 97
Rice
  Golden Rice, 92
  Mexican Pilaf, 94

Mexican Rice, 93
Rice Pudding, 131
White Rice, 91
Roasted and Marinated Chili Strips, 37
Romaine with Creamy Roquefort Dressing
and Cornmeal Chili Strips, 107

Salad dressings
Creamy Roquefort Dressing, 107
Mint Vinaigrette, 105
Salads
Black Bean Salad, 109
Cactus Paddle Salad, 110
Chickpea Salad, 112
Mexican Potato Salad, 115
Romaine with Creamy Roquefort Dressing
and Cornmeal Chili Strips, 107
Spinach Salad with Pine Nuts, Cheese,
and Mint Vinaigrette, 105
Salsas and sauces
Cherry Tomato Salsa, 124
Cooked Green Salsa, 29
Corn and Sweet Red Pepper Salsa, 36
Fresh Tomatillo Salsa, 28
Fresh Tomato Salsa, 24
Grapefruit and Pumpkin Seed Salsa, 35
Guacamole, 20
Jícama and Watermelon Salsa, 33
Melon Jalapeño Salsa, 34
Mole Verde, 55
Papaya and Peanut Salsa, 35
Piquant Sauce with Chipotle Chilies and Tamarind, 30
Red Enchilada Sauce, 57
Salsa Ranchera, 25
salsas verdes, 28–29
Smoky Tomato Ketchup, 31
Strawberry Mango Sauce, 138
Salt, Chili, 19
Sautéed Chili Strips, 116
Savory Chickpea and Walnut Empanada Filling, 61
Seeds
about, 12
Grapefruit and Pumpkin Seed Salsa, 35

Mole Verde, 55
Toasted Pumpkin Seeds, 21
toasting, 14
Shredded Cabbage or Lettuce, 23
Simmered Vegetable Tacos, 58
Smoky Tomato Ketchup, 31
Soups and chowders
Avocado Vichyssoise, 79
Corn Chowder, 74
Green *Pozole*, 75
Lentil and Chard Soup, 71
Melon and Potato Soup, 78
Mexican Gazpacho, 81
Squash Blossom Soup, 76
Toasted Garlic Soup, 72
Tortilla Soup, 70
Spaghetti a la Primavera Mexicana, 90
Spaghetti with Spinach, Chilies, Cream, and Almonds, 85
Spices
about, 12
toasting, 14
Spinach
Spaghetti with Spinach, Chilies, Cream, and Almonds, 85
Spinach Salad with Pine Nuts, Cheese,
and Mint Vinaigrette, 105
Squash
Candied Gourd Squash, 141
Chayote Stewed with Tomatoes, Raisins,
and White Wine, 117
Spaghetti a la Primavera Mexicana, 90
Stuffed Chayote with Peanuts and Dressed Cilantro, 120
Squash Blossom Soup, 76
Stew, Fava Bean, 100
Stock, Vegetable, 69
Strawberry Mango Sauce, 138
Stuffed Chayote with Peanuts and Dressed Cilantro, 120
Sweet Nut Tamales with Strawberry Mango Sauce, 136
Swiss chard
Lentil and Chard Soup, 71

Tacos, Simmered Vegetable, 58
Tamales
Black Bean and Plantain Tamale Filling, 65

Creamed Corn and Cheese Tamale Filling, 65
Nut Filling for Sweet Tamales, 138
Savory Tamales, 64–65
Sweet Nut Tamales with Strawberry Mango Sauce, 136
Toasted Garlic Soup, 72
Toasted Pumpkin Seeds, 21
Tomatillos
  about, 14
  Cooked Green Salsa, 29
  Fresh Tomatillo Salsa, 28
  Green *Pozole*, 75
  Mole Verde, 55
  Piquant Sauce with Chipotle Chilies and Tamarind, 30
Tomatoes
  Chayote Stewed with Tomatoes, Raisins,
    and White Wine, 117
  Cherry Tomato Salsa, 124
  Chilaquiles, 59
  Fresh Tomato Salsa, 24
  Mexican Gazpacho, 81
  Piquant Sauce with Chipotle Chilies and Tamarind, 30
  preparing, 14
  Red Enchilada Sauce, 57
  Salsa Ranchera, 25
  Smoky Tomato Ketchup, 31
  Vermicelli with Tomatoes and Chipotle Chilies, 87
Tortillas
  Chilaquiles, 59
  Corn Tortillas, 45
  Flour Tortillas, 48
  Green Enchiladas in Mole Verde, 55
  Quesadillas, 52
  Red Enchiladas, 56
  Simmered Vegetable Tacos, 58
  Tortilla Chips, 49
  Tortilla Soup, 70
Tostada, Unclassic, 63

Vegetables. *See also* individual vegetables
  Mexican Crudités, 22–23
  Pickled Mixed Vegetables, 38
  Simmered Vegetable Tacos, 58
  Vegetable Stock, 69

Vegetarian Mixed Grill Feast, 125–26
Vermicelli with Tomatoes and Chipotle Chilies, 87
Vinegar, Fruit, 12–13

Watermelon Salsa, Jícama and, 33
Wedding Cookies, 146
Well-fried Beans with Cheese and Fresh Red Chilies, 97
White Rice, 91
Wilted Red Onions, 22

TABLE OF EQUIVALENTS

❋

THE EXACT EQUIVALENTS IN THE FOLLOWING TABLES HAVE

BEEN ROUNDED FOR CONVENIENCE.

US/UK

oz=ounce
lb=pound
in=inch
ft=foot
tbl=tablespoon
fl oz=fluid ounce
qt=quart

METRIC

g=gram
kg=kilogram
mm=millimeter
cm=centimeter
ml=milliliter
l=liter

WEIGHTS

US/UK	Metric
1 oz	30 g
2 oz	60 g
3 oz	90 g
4 oz (¼ lb)	125 g
5 oz (⅓ lb)	155 g
6 oz	185 g
7 oz	220 g
8 oz (½ lb)	250 g
10 oz	315 g
12 oz (¾ lb)	375 g
14 oz	440 g
16 oz (1 lb)	500 g
1½ lb	750 g
2 lb	1 kg
3 lb	1.5 kg

OVEN TEMPERATURES

Fahrenheit	Celsius	Gas
250	20	½
275	140	1
300	150	2
325	160	3
350	180	4
375	190	5
400	200	6
425	220	7
450	230	8
475	240	9
500	260	10

LIQUIDS

US	Metric	UK
2 tbl	30 ml	1 fl oz
¼ cup	60 ml	2 fl oz
⅓ cup	80 ml	3 fl oz
½ cup	125 ml	4 fl oz
⅔ cup	160 ml	5 fl oz
¾ cup	180 ml	6 fl oz
1 cup	250 ml	8 fl oz
1½ cups	75 ml	12 fl oz
2 cups	500 ml	16 fl oz
4 cups/1 qt	1 l	32 fl oz

LENGTH MEASURES

⅛ in	3 mm
¼ in	6 mm
½ in	12 mm
1 in	2.5 cm
2 in	5 cm
3 in	7.5 cm
4 in	10 cm
5 in	13 cm
6 in	15 cm
7 in	18 cm
8 in	20 cm
9 in	23 cm
10 in	25 cm
11 in	28 cm
12/1 ft	30 cm

All-purpose (plain) flour/ dried bread crumbs/chopped nuts

¼ cup	1 oz	30 g
⅓ cup	1½ oz	45 g
½ cup	2 oz	60 g
¾ cup	3 oz	90 g
1 cup	4 oz	125 g
1½ cups	6 oz	185 g
2 cups	8 oz	250 g

Whole-Wheat (Wholemeal) Flour

3 tbl	1 oz	30 g
½ cup	2 oz	60 g
⅔ cup	3 oz	90 g
1 cup	4 oz	125 g
1¼ cups	5 oz	155 g
1⅔ cups	7 oz	210 g
1¾ cups	8 oz	250 g

Brown Sugar

¼ cup	1½ oz	45 g
½ cup	3 oz	90 g
¾ cup	4 oz	125 g
1 cup	5½ oz	170 g
1½ cups	8 oz	250 g
2 cups	10 oz	315 g

White Sugar

¼ cup	2 oz	60 g
⅓ cup	3 oz	90 g
½ cup	4 oz	125 g
¾ cup	6 oz	185 g
1 cup	8 oz	250 g
1½ cups	12 oz	375 g
2 cups	1 lb	500 g

Raisins/Currants/Semolina

¼ cup	1 oz	30 g
⅓ cup	2 oz	60 g
½ cup	3 oz	90 g
¾ cup	4 oz	125 g
1 cup	5 oz	155 g

Long-Grain Rice/Cornmeal

⅓ cup	2 oz	60 g
½ cup	2½ oz	75 g
¾ cup	4 oz	125 g
1 cup	5 oz	155 g
1½ cups	8 oz	250 g

Dried Beans

¼ cup	1½ oz	45 g
⅓ cup	2 oz	60 g
½ cup	3 oz	90 g
¾ cup	5 oz	155 g
1 cup	6 oz	185 g
1¼ cups	8 oz	250 g
1½ cups	12 oz	375 g

Rolled Oats

⅓ cup	1 oz	30 g
⅔ cup	2 oz	60 g
1 cup	3 oz	90 g
1½ cups	4 oz	125 g
2 cups	5 oz	155 g

Jam/Honey

2 tbl	2 oz	60 g
¼ cup	3 oz	90 g
½ cup	5 oz	155 g
¾ cup	8 oz	250 g
1 cup	11 oz	345 g

Grated Parmesan/Romano Cheese

¼ cup	1 oz	30 g
½ cup	2 oz	60 g
¾ cup	3 oz	90 g
1 cup	4 oz	125 g
1⅓ cups	5 oz	155 g
2 cups	7 oz	220 g